QUALITATIVE RESEARCH DESIGN

Applied Social Research Methods Series
Volume 41

APPLIED SOCIAL RESEARCH METHODS SERIES

Series Editors
LEONARD BICKMAN, Peabody College, Vanderbilt University, Nashville
DEBRA J. ROG, Vanderbilt University, Washington, DC

Other volumes in this series are listed at the end of the book

QUALITATIVE RESEARCH DESIGN

An Interactive Approach

Joseph A. Maxwell

Applied Social Research Methods Series
Volume 41

SAGE Publications
International Educational and Professional Publisher
Thousand Oaks   London   New Delhi

For information address:

SAGE Publications, Inc.
2455 Teller Road
Thousand Oaks, California 91320
E-mail: order@sagepub.com

SAGE Publications Ltd.
6 Bonhill Street
London EC2A 4PU
United Kingdom

SAGE Publications India Pvt. Ltd.
M-32 Market
Greater Kailash I
New Delhi 110 048 India

Printed in the United States of America

Maxwell, Joseph Alex, 1941-
    Qualitative research design: An interactive approach / author,
Joseph A. Maxwell.
        p. cm.—(Applied social research methods series)
    Includes bibliographical references and index.
    ISBN 0-8039-7328-4 (acid-free paper).—ISBN 0-8039-7329-2 (pbk.:
acid-free paper)
    1. Research—Methodology. I. Title. II. Series.
Q180.55.M4M39 1996
001.4'2—dc20   95-50209

This book is printed on acid-free paper.

96 97 98 99   10 9 8 7 6 5 4 3 2

Sage Production Editor: Gillian Dickens

Contents

Preface

Contrary to what you may have heard,
qualitative research designs do exist.

Miles & Huberman, 1994, p. 16

A review of a book on wines that I once read stated that "a guidebook is best when those guiding you are opinionated," and I have attempted to meet that standard. This book is not a lowest-common-denominator compendium of conventional wisdom. I have definite views on qualitative research design, and a major part of my motivation for writing this book is that I believe that much of what has been written about research design is inconsistent with the way qualitative researchers actually go about designing their research.

I have therefore tried to present an approach to qualitative research design that both captures what qualitative researchers really do, and provides support and guidance for those embarking for the first time on designing a qualitative study. This book is intended to provide advice on every part of the design process: figuring out what your study should accomplish, constructing a theoretical framework, developing research questions, deciding on your strategies and methods for data collection and analysis, and planning how to deal with potential validity threats to your conclusions.

Many students (and some experienced researchers) believe that their research *proposal,* rather than the design of their study, is the major hurdle they face in preparing for their dissertations or in seeking funding. They see qualitative research design as largely common sense, something that doesn't require systematic planning or new ways of thinking. Writing a successful proposal, on the other hand, is viewed as a mysterious and difficult task, requiring them to find the right formula or language that will get their study accepted or funded.

As a result of teaching a course on qualitative research design and proposal writing for the past 7 years, I have come to believe the opposite: that design is by far the more difficult of the two tasks. Most students in my course discover that they need to substantially rethink and develop their research designs in order to make them consistent and workable, and that this process can force them to reexamine some of their basic assumptions about their topic and study. On the other hand, once they have worked out their research designs more clearly, writing a proposal is not nearly as intimidating or difficult a task as they had feared.

There is a folktale about a boy who was driving a cartload of apples to market. As he had never been to this market before, he asked an old man standing by the road how long it would take to get there. The old man looked at the cart, then looked at the road, and finally said, "About 3 hours, but if you hurry, it will take you all day." The boy, thinking to himself, "What does he know?" whipped up the horse and set off at a fast pace. Soon the cart hit a bump in the road, and many of the apples were knocked out. It took a while for the boy to pick them all up, and because he felt he was late, he now drove even faster. Soon the cart hit another bump, even more apples fell out, and proceeding in this way, it took the boy all day to get to market.

The moral of this story is that if you rush into writing your proposal before you have your design clearly conceptualized, it may substantially slow your progress.[1] Peters (1992) provides a cautionary tale of a student who attempted this and wasted a year's worth of work; he comments that the student "should have realized that the reason he couldn't create a clear proposal was that there were basic flaws with the conception of his thesis" (pp. 196-197).

Successfully developing both your research design and your proposal requires that you have a clear understanding of the difference between the two. Your *design* is the logic and coherence of your research study—the components of your research and the ways in which these relate to one another. Your proposal, on the other hand, is a *document* that communicates and justifies this design to a particular audience. Creating these two things are different tasks, and treating them as if they were identical, as some books on research design do, can make both design and proposal writing more difficult than necessary.

For these reasons, this book focuses primarily on research design, rather than on proposal writing. However, there are important connections between design and proposal structure. I highlight these connections throughout the book, and in Chapter 7, I discuss how to make the transition from *designing* a study to *proposing* it. The model of research design that this book presents is partly drawn from the structure of qualitative research proposals and is thus directly useful in proposal writing.

I've written this book to be useful both to people who are just beginning to plan a qualitative study and to those who are already involved in a qualitative research project. If you're thinking about or preparing for a qualitative study, you can use the book to develop a research design and proposal. If you're already engaged in a qualitative study, you can use it to reconceptualize what you're doing, focus the study, identify potential problems and solutions, and develop more useful and relevant theory; that is, to modify your design or to make this design more explicit.

I believe that research design, like most things, is best learned by doing it, and I've tried to incorporate a "hands on" approach to design in this book. Thus, in order for the book to be most useful to you, you should have a qualitative research project in mind that you're either planning to do or are now engaged in. You don't need to have the details of your study worked out—that's what this book should help you to do—but you do need to have a definite topic or subject and some idea of the relevant research and theory on this topic.

The model of design that I present here derives primarily from my experience in teaching qualitative research methods for 10 years at the Harvard Graduate School of Education; from the 6 years that I was a member of the school's Committee on Degrees, which reviews all qualifying paper and dissertation proposals submitted by doctoral students; and from what I have learned in supervising qualitative studies and helping students with their proposals. I've also drawn insight and examples from my own research and proposal writing. My original training was in social and cultural anthropology, at the University of Chicago, but my work has covered a wide range of approaches and topics, from traditional ethnography to qualitative program evaluation and applied research on medical education.

There are far too many people who have contributed to the writing of this book to thank them individually, but I particularly want to acknowledge:

Carol Weiss, who first suggested that I write this book, and has been a steady supporter during the writing process

The students who, over the last 7 years, worked with me as Teaching Fellows in a course on qualitative research design: Maria Broderick, Ana Maria Garcia Blanco, Isabel Londoño, Barbara Miller, Carla Rensenbrink, Anna Romer, Clarissa Sawyer, Janie Simmons, Rachel Sing, Marydee Spillett, and Connie Titone. Most of what is in this book emerged from or was substantially reshaped by our weekly discussions of research design and students' difficulties in learning this. In addition, many of them read early portions or drafts of the book and provided critical feedback on what worked and what didn't.

Martha Regan-Smith, for permission to use her dissertation proposal as an example, and Suman Bhattacharjea, Maria Broderick, Brendan Croskery, Beatrice Guilbault, Gail Lenehan, Isabel Londoño, Jane Margolis, and Bobby Starnes for permission to use examples from their research in this book

Cynthia Chataway, Loren Faibisch, Beatrice Guilbault, Michael Huberman, Susan Moore Johnson, Sue Malspeis, Matthew Miles, Richard Murnane, Carol Pelletier, Annie Rogers, Ellen Snee, Meg Turner, Robert Weiss, and anyone whom I've forgotten to name, who gave me useful comments on earlier drafts

All of the students in my course on qualitative research design, who have been the guinea pigs for earlier versions of the presentations and exercises included here, and who have given me a great deal of valuable feedback on these materials

Meg Turner, for suggesting the subtitle "An Interactive Approach"

C. Deborah Laughton at Sage Publications, and the editors for this series, Len Bickman and Debra Rog, for valuable feedback and encouragement, and for prodding me to stop revising the book and get it out the door

Charity Boudouris and Wilson Manoharan for uncomplainingly copying endless drafts of this book to distribute to students and colleagues

Helen Silver, for preparing the index, and Elaine Gampp and Eph Weiss, for help with the artwork

NOTE

1. I am not repeating the fallacy that you should have your argument worked out in your head before you put it on paper; see Becker (1986) for an eloquent refutation of this approach. Working out your design will involve a substantial amount of writing, because, as Becker points out, writing is thinking. However, much of it is a different *sort* of writing from what you will actually put in the proposal; trying to begin by writing something that will persuade an audience of critical reviewers can seriously interfere with the sorts of thinking you need to do to design your study.

1

A Model for Qualitative Research Design

In 1625, Gustavus II Adolphus, the king of Sweden, commissioned the construction of four warships to further his imperialistic goals. The most ambitious of these ships, named the *Vasa,* was one of the largest warships of its time, with 64 cannons arrayed in two gundecks. On August 10, 1628, the *Vasa,* resplendent in its brightly painted and gilded woodwork, was launched in Stockholm harbor with cheering crowds and considerable ceremony. But the cheering was short-lived; caught by a gust of wind while still in the harbor, the ship suddenly heeled over, foundered, and sank.

An investigation was immediately ordered, and it became apparent that the ballast compartment had not been made large enough to balance the two gundecks that the king had specified. With only 121 tons of stone ballast, the ship lacked stability. However, if the builders had simply added more ballast, the lower gundeck would have been brought dangerously close to the water; the ship lacked the buoyancy to accommodate that much weight.

In more abstract terms, the *design* of the *Vasa*—the ways in which the different components of the ship were planned and constructed to interrelate with one another—was fatally flawed. The ship was carefully built, meeting all of the existing standards for solid workmanship, but key characteristics of its different parts—in particular, the weight of the gundecks and ballast and the size of the hold—were not compatible, and the interaction of these characteristics caused the ship to capsize. Shipbuilders of that day did not have a general theory of ship design; they worked primarily from traditional models and by trial and error and had no way to calculate stability. Apparently, the *Vasa* was originally planned as a smaller ship and was then scaled up, at the king's insistence, to add the second gundeck, leaving too little room in the hold (Kvarning, 1993).

The tragedy of the *Vasa* illustrates the general concept of design that I am using here: "an underlying scheme that governs functioning, developing, or unfolding" and "the arrangement of elements or details in a product or work of art" (*Merriam-Webster's Collegiate Dictionary*). A good design, one in which the components work harmoniously together, promotes efficient and successful functioning; a flawed design leads to poor operation or failure.

Surprisingly, most works dealing with *research* design use a different conception of design: "a plan or protocol for carrying out or accomplishing something (esp. a scientific experiment)" (*Merriam-Webster's Collegiate Dictionary*). They present design as a series of stages or tasks in planning or conducting a study. Although some versions of this view of design are circular and recursive, all are essentially linear in the sense of being a one-directional *sequence* of steps, from problem formulation to conclusions or theory. The implication of these models is that there is a single optimal order for the different components or tasks in conducting a study, although this sequence may be repeated.[1]

Grady and Wallston (1988, p. 10) refer to this sequential approach to design as the traditional model. In opposition to this model, they present what Martin (1982) has called the "garbage can" model of research design. The latter model is based on Cohen, March, and Olsen's (1972) influential garbage-can model of organizational decision making, which was a reaction to the prevalent rational and linear models of how decisions get made. Grady and Wallston (1988) emphasize the essentially contingent and nonlinear nature of design decisions:

> In Martin's model, four elements swirl around in the garbage can or decision space of the particular research project. These elements are theories, methods, resources, and solutions.... The key to Martin's model is not the creation of these elements, but their interdependence and coequal status in the model. Each influences the others and each is a major factor in the outcome of the research. (p. 12)

Grady and Wallston's revised model, which they call Garbage Can II, adds additional elements to the decision space, including problems, phenomena, and the personal concerns of the researcher (pp. 12-13).

Whatever advantages the traditional, sequential model may have for quantitative research,[2] it doesn't adequately represent the logic and process of qualitative research, in which each component of the design may need to be reconsidered or modified in response to new developments or to changes in some other component. In a qualitative study, "research design should be a reflexive process operating through every stage of a project" (Hammersley & Atkinson, 1983, p. 28). The activities of collecting and analyzing data, developing and modifying theory, elaborating or refocusing the research questions, and identifying and eliminating validity threats are usually all going on more or less simultaneously, each influencing all of the others.

This conception of design is exemplified in a classic qualitative study of medical students (Becker, Geer, Hughes, & Strauss, 1961/1977). The authors begin their chapter on the "Design of the Study" by stating that

> in one sense, our study had no design. That is, we had no well-worked-out set of hypotheses to be tested, no data-gathering instruments purposely designed to secure information relevant to these hypotheses, no set of analytic procedures specified in advance. Insofar as the term *design* implies these features of elaborate prior planning, our study had none.
>
> If we take the idea of design in a larger and looser sense, using it to identify those elements of order, system, and consistency our procedures did exhibit, our study had a design. We can say what this was by describing our original view of the problem, our theoretical and methodological commitments, and the way these affected our research and were affected by it as we proceeded. (p. 17)

Like the garbage can model, the model of qualitative research design that I present in this book emphasizes that research design does not begin from a fixed starting point or proceed through a determinate sequence of steps, and it recognizes the importance of interconnection and interaction among the different design components. However, the conception of the design components "swirling around" in an undefined space does not do justice to some particularly important connections between components. It also provides little explicit guidance to the researcher in figuring out how to proceed in developing a design or how to effectively communicate this design in a proposal.

For these reasons, the model I use in this book, which I call an *interactive* model, does have a definite structure. However, it is an interconnected and flexible structure. This book identifies the key components in a design and the relationships among these and presents a strategy for creating coherent and workable relationships among these components. It also provides an explicit plan for moving from your design to a research proposal.

This interactive model does not dismiss the importance of design but reinforces it. Research design is like a philosophy of life; no one is without one, but some people are more aware of theirs, and thus able to make more informed and consistent decisions. Yin (1994) states that "every type of empirical research has an implicit, if not explicit, research design" (p. 19). Because a design always exists, it is important to *make* it explicit, to get it out in the open where its strengths, limitations, and implications can be clearly understood.

Design in qualitative research is an iterative process that involves "tacking" (Geertz, 1976, p. 235) back and forth between the different components of the design, assessing the implications of purposes, theory, research questions, methods, and validity threats for one another.[3] Such an interactive model is more compatible with the definition of design as the arrangement of elements governing the functioning of a study than it is with design as a preestablished plan for carrying out the study or as a sequence of steps in conducting that study. This book is therefore based on a conception of research design as the underlying structure and interconnection of the components of the study and the implications of each component for the others.

The model I present here has five components. These components can be characterized by the issues that each is intended to address:

1. *Purposes:* What are the ultimate goals of this study? What issues is it intended to illuminate, and what practices will it influence? Why do you want to conduct it, and why should we care about the results? Why is the study worth doing?

2. *Conceptual Context:* What do you think is going on with the phenomena you plan to study? What theories, findings, and conceptual frameworks relating to these phenomena will guide or inform your study, and what literature, preliminary research, and personal experience will you draw on? This component of the design contains the *theory* that you already have or are developing about the setting or issues that you are studying. There are four main sources for this theory: your own experience, existing theory and research, the results of any pilot studies or preliminary research that you've done, and thought experiments.

3. *Research Questions:* What, specifically, do you want to understand by doing this study? What do you *not* know about the phenomena you are studying that you want to learn? What questions will your research attempt to answer, and how are these questions related to one another?

4. *Methods:* What will you actually do in conducting this study? What approaches and techniques will you use to collect and analyze your data, and how do these constitute an integrated strategy? This component of your design includes four main parts: your research relationship with the people you study, your site selection and sampling decisions, your data collection methods, and the data analysis techniques you will use.

5. *Validity:* How might you be wrong? What are the plausible alternative explanations and validity threats to the potential conclusions of your study, and how will you deal with these? How do the data that you have, or that

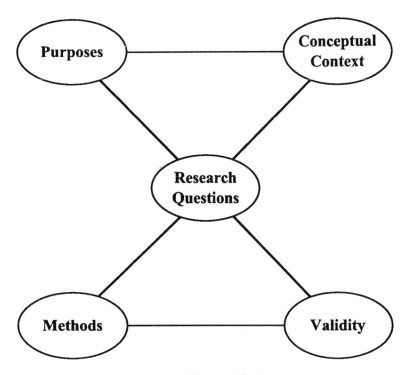

Figure 1.1. An Interactive Model of Research Design

you could collect, support or challenge your ideas about what's going on? Why should we believe your results?

These components are not radically different from the ones presented in many other discussions of research design (e.g., LeCompte & Preissle, 1993; Miles & Huberman, 1994; Robson, 1993). What is innovative is the relationships among the components. In this model, the components form an integrated and interacting whole, with each component closely tied to several others, rather than being linked in a linear or cyclic sequence. The key relationships among the components are displayed in Figure 1.1.

This diagram presents the relationships among the five components of a qualitative design as an hourglass figure. The lines between the components represent two-way ties of influence or implication. Although there are also connections other than those emphasized here (e.g., between purposes and methods and between conceptual context and validity), the ones shown are generally the most important.

The upper triangle of this hourglass model should be a closely integrated unit. Your research questions should have a clear relationship to the purposes of your study and should be informed by what is already known about the phenomena you are studying and the theoretical tools that can be applied to these phenomena. In addition, the purposes of the study should be informed by current theory and knowledge, whereas the choice of relevant theory and knowledge depends on the purposes and questions.

Similarly, the bottom triangle of the model should also be closely integrated. The methods you use must enable you to answer your research questions and also to deal with plausible validity threats to these answers. The questions, in turn, need to be framed so as to take the feasibility of the methods and the seriousness of particular validity threats into account, whereas the plausibility and relevance of particular validity threats depend on the questions and methods chosen.

The top part of the model is the external aspect of the design; it includes the goals, experiences, knowledge, assumptions, and theory that you bring to the study and incorporate in the design. The bottom part is the internal aspect; it includes the actual activities that you will carry out and the processes that you will go through to develop and test your conclusions. The research questions are the center, or hub, of the model; they connect these two halves of the design and should inform, and be sensitive to, all of the other components.

The connections among the different components of the model are not rigid rules or fixed implications; they allow for a certain amount of "give" and elasticity in the design. I find it useful to think of them as rubber bands. They can stretch and bend to some extent, but they exert a definite tension on different parts of the design, and beyond a particular point, or under certain stresses, they will break. This metaphor represents a qualitative design as something with considerable flexibility, but in which the different parts impose constraints on each other, constraints that, if violated, make the design ineffective.

There are many other factors besides these five components that will influence the design of your study, as the garbage can models described earlier suggest; these include your resources, research abilities, perceived problems, ethical standards, the research setting, and the data you collect. In my view, these are not part of the *design* of a study, but either belong to the *environment* within which the research and its design exist or are *products* of the research. You will need to take these factors into account in designing your study, just as the design of a ship needs to take into account the kinds of wind and waves it will encounter and the sorts of cargo it will carry. Figure 1.2 presents some of the factors in the environment that

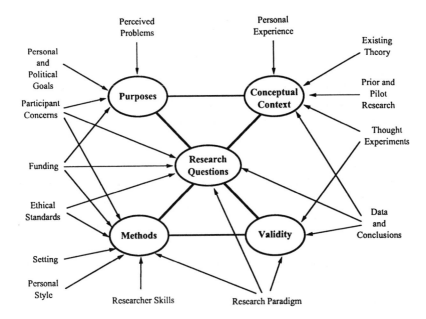

Figure 1.2. Contextual Factors Influencing a Research Design

can influence the design and conduct of a study and displays some of the key linkages of these factors with components of the research design. These factors and linkages will be discussed in subsequent chapters.

I want to say something specifically about ethics, because I have not identified it as a separate component of research design. This isn't because I don't think ethics is important for qualitative design; on the contrary, attention to ethical issues in qualitative research is being increasingly recognized as essential (Deyhle, Hess, & LeCompte, 1992; Eisner & Peshkin, 1990, pp. 243-299; Kimmel, 1988; Punch, 1986). Instead, it is because I believe that ethical concerns should be involved in *every* aspect of design. I have particularly tried to address these concerns in relation to methods, but they are also relevant to your purposes, the selection of research questions, validity concerns, and the critical assessment of theory.

As the subtitle of the book indicates, my approach to design is an interactive one. It is interactive in three senses. First, the design model itself is interactive; each of the components has implications for the other components, rather than the components being in a linear, one-directional relationship with one another. Second, the design of a qualitative study should be able to change in interaction with the situation in which the study is conducted, rather than simply being a fixed determinant of research practice. (Example 1.1 illustrates both of these interactive processes in the evolution of the design of one study.) Finally, the learning process embodied in this book is interactive, with frequent opportunities for you to engage in the design of your own study. This book does not simply present abstract research design principles that you can memorize and then later use in your research. You *will* learn generalizable principles, but you'll learn these best by creating a design for a particular qualitative project.

I do not believe that there is one right model for research design. However, I think that the model that I present here is a useful model for two main reasons:

1. It explicitly identifies as *components* of design the key issues about which you will need to make decisions, and which will need to be addressed in your research proposal. These components are therefore less likely to be ignored and can be dealt with in a systematic manner.

2. It emphasizes the *interactive* nature of design decisions in qualitative research and the multiple connections among design components. A common reason that proposals are rejected is because they do not explicitly present the logical connections between the design components, and the model I present here makes it easier to address these connections.

A good design for your study, like a good design for a ship, will help it to safely and efficiently reach its destination. A poor design, one in which the components are not well-connected or are incompatible, will at best be inefficient, and at worst will fail to achieve its goals.

THE ORGANIZATION OF THIS BOOK

This book is structured to guide you through the process of designing a qualitative study. It highlights the issues for which design decisions must be made, and it presents some of the considerations that should inform these decisions. As the model illustrates, it is based on an interactive understanding of the components of design, rather than on a sequence of stages or actions.

Each chapter in the book deals with one component of design, and these form a logical sequence. However, this organization is only a conceptual and presentation device, not a procedure to follow in designing an actual study. You should make decisions about each component in light of your thinking about all of the other components, and you may need to modify

EXAMPLE 1.1

The Evolution of a Research Design

Maria Broderick began her dissertation study of a hospital-based support group for cancer patients with a theoretical background in adult psychological development and experience in the design of such programs; an interest in discovering how patients' perceptions of support and interaction within the group were related to their developmental level; a plan to use observation, interviews, and developmental tests to answer this question; and the goals of improving such programs and developing a career in clinical practice. However, after her proposal was approved, she lost access to the group she had originally planned to study and was unable to find another suitable cancer program. She ended up negotiating permission to study a stress-reduction program for patients in a hospital setting, but she was not allowed to observe the classes; in addition, the program team insisted on a quasi-experimental research design. This forced her to both broaden her theoretical context beyond cancer-support programs to behavioral medicine programs in general and to alter her methods to rely primarily on pre- and postinterviews and developmental tests.

As Maria was beginning her research, however, she herself was diagnosed with a stress-related illness. This had a major effect on the research design. First, she gained access to the program as a patient and discovered that it wasn't actually run as a support program, but in a traditional classroom format. This made her extensive literature review on support groups largely irrelevant. Second, she found that her own experiences of her illness and what seemed to help her deal with stress differed substantially from what was reported in the literature. These two developments profoundly altered her conceptual context and research questions, shifting her theoretical focus from ego development to cognitive development, adult learning, and educational theory. In addition, she found that pretesting of the patients was impossible for practical reasons, eliminating the possibility of quasi-experimental assessment of patient changes and shifting her methods and validity checks back toward her original plans.

While Maria was analyzing her data, her gradual creation of a theory that made sense of these patients' (and her own) experiences directed her to new bodies of literature and theoretical approaches. Her increasing focus on what the patients *learned* through the program caused her to see meditation and cognitive restructuring as tools for reshaping one's view of stress, and this focus led her to develop a broader view of stress as a cultural phenomenon. It also reconnected her with her longtime interest in nontraditional education for adults. Finally, these changes influenced a shift in her career goals from clinical practice to an academic position, and her purposes for the study came to emphasize relating adult developmental theory to empowerment curricula and improving adult education in nontraditional settings.

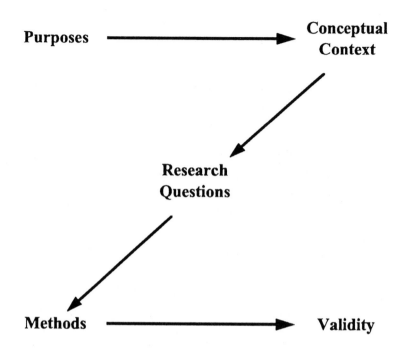

Figure 1.3. The Organization of This Book

previous design decisions in response to new information or changes in your thinking.

This book will take a Z-shaped path (Figure 1.3) through the components of this model, beginning with purposes (Chapter 2). The purposes of your study are not only important, but primary; if your reasons for doing the study aren't clear, it can be difficult to make any decisions about the rest of the design. Your conceptual context (Chapter 3) will be discussed next, both because it should connect closely to your purposes and because the purposes and context jointly have a major influence on the formulation of research questions for the study. Your research questions (Chapter 4) are thus a logical next topic; these three components should form a coherent unit.

The next component to be discussed is methods (Chapter 5): how you will actually collect and analyze the data to answer your research questions. However, these methods and answers need to be connected to issues of validity (Chapter 6): how you might be wrong, and what would make your answers more believable than alternative answers. Research questions, methods, and validity also should form an integrated unit in which the methods for obtaining answers to the questions, as well as the means for assuring the credibility of the potential answers in the face of plausible validity threats, are clearly conceptualized and linked to the research questions. Finally, Chapter 7 discusses the implications of my model of design for developing research proposals and provides a map showing how to get from one to the other.

THE EXERCISES IN THIS BOOK

C. Wright-Mills (1959) says that

> One of the very worst things that happens to social scientists is that they feel the need to write of their "plans" on only one occasion: when they are going to ask for money for a specific piece of work or "a project." It is as a request for funds that most planning is done, or at least carefully written about. However standard the practice, I think this very bad: it is bound in some degree to be salesmanship, and, given prevailing expectations, very likely to result in painstaking pretensions; the project is likely to be "presented," rounded out in some manner long before it ought to be; it is often a contrived thing, aimed at getting the money for ulterior purposes, however valuable, as well as for the research presented. A practicing social scientist ought periodically to review "the state of my problems and plans." (p. 197)

Mills goes on to make an eloquent plea that each researcher write regularly and systematically about his or her research, "just for himself and perhaps for discussion with friends" (p. 198), and keep a file of these writings, which qualitative researchers usually call *memos*.

All of the exercises in this book are memos of one form or another, and I want to briefly discuss the nature of memos and how to use them effectively. The memo (sometimes called *analytic memo*) is an extremely versatile tool that can be used for many different purposes. It refers to any writing that a researcher does in relationship to the research other than actual fieldnotes, transcription, or coding. A memo can range from a brief marginal comment on a transcript or a theoretical idea recorded in a field journal to a full-fledged analytic essay. What all of these have in common is that they are ways of getting ideas down on paper (or on a computer disk) and of using this writing as a way to facilitate reflection and analytic insight. Many of the examples in this book are memos, or are based on memos.

Memos do for ideas what fieldnotes and transcripts do for perception: they convert thought into a form that allows examination and further manipulation. When your thoughts are recorded in memos, you can code and file them, just as you do your fieldnotes and interview transcripts, and return to them to develop the ideas further. Not writing memos is the research equivalent of having Alzheimer's disease; you may not remember your important insights when you need them.[4]

Memos are one of the most important techniques you have for developing your own ideas. You should therefore think of memos as a way to help you *understand* your topic, setting, or study, not just as a way of recording or presenting an understanding you've already reached. Memos should include reflections on your reading and ideas, as well as your fieldwork. Write memos as a way of working on a problem you have in making sense of your topic, setting, or study. Write memos whenever you have an idea that you want to develop further, or simply to record the idea for later development. Write *lots* of memos, throughout the course of your research project; remember that in qualitative research, design is something that goes on during the entire study, not just at the beginning. Memos can be written on methodological issues, ethics, personal reactions, or anything else about your study. Think of memos as a kind of decentralized field journal; if you prefer, you can write your memos in an actual journal.

Whatever form these memos take, their value depends on two things. The first is that you engage in serious reflection and self-critique, rather than just mechanically recording events and thoughts. The second is that you organize your memos in a systematic, retrievable form, so that the observations and insights can easily be accessed for future examination. I do my own reflection primarily in two forms: on 3×5 cards, which I always carry with me for jotting down ideas and which I index by date and topic, and in computer files relating to particular projects, which I use for longer memos. During my dissertation research in an Inuit community in northern Canada, I also kept a field journal, which was invaluable in making sense of my personal responses to the research situation. It can also be very useful to share some of your memos with colleagues or fellow students for their feedback.[5]

Although memos are primarily a tool for thinking, they can also serve as an initial draft of material that you will later incorporate (with substantial revision) in a proposal, report, or publication, and I've tried to design most of the memo exercises in this book so that they can be used in this way. However, thinking of memos primarily as a way of communicating to *other* people will inevitably interfere with the kind of reflective writing that you need to do to make memos most useful to you. Beware of what Becker

(1986) calls "classy writing"—language that is intended to impress rather than clarify. A saying among writing instructors is "When you write, don't put a tuxedo on your brain" (Metzger, 1993, p. 16).

NOTES

1. A third definition treats designs as discrete, standard arrangements of research methods that have their own coherence and logic, as possible answers to the question, What research design are you using? For example, a randomized, double-blind experiment is one research design; a qualitative case study is another. For several reasons, this conception of design is not particularly helpful in qualitative research. First, few qualitative studies lend themselves to such "off-the-rack" approaches; as discussed throughout this book, qualitative design needs to be inductive and flexible. Second, standardized designs generally deal explicitly only with methods and don't address the other components of design (in my model, purposes, context, questions, and validity) or the relationships among these.

2. The advantages are debatable. Grady and Wallston (1988) state that the traditional, sequential model "presents an idealized picture of the process that is far different from how research is *actually* conducted" (p. 11), and is particularly inappropriate for applied research, which can start from a variety of different points and "requires an entirely different model of the research process than the traditional one offered in most textbooks" (p. 10).

3. This tacking back and forth is similar in some ways to the hermeneutic circle of textual interpretation. However, my commitment to an interactive rather than a sequential model of research design does not derive from any adherence to an interpretive or humanistic rather than a scientific paradigm for research; these two distinctions are separate issues. The interactive model I present here is drawn to a significant extent from research practices in the natural sciences, particularly biology, and I would argue that it is applicable (with modifications) to quantitative as well as qualitative research. In contrast, Janesick (1994), who sees qualitative research design as an interpretive art form analogous to dance, nevertheless states that "qualitative research design begins with a question" (p. 210) and presents research design as a sequence of decisions that the researcher will need to make at each stage of the research.

4. For additional discussions of what a memo involves, see Miles and Huberman (1994, pp. 72-75), Bogdan and Biklen (1992, pp. 121-124), and Mills (1959). More detailed information on memos can be found in Schatzman and Strauss (1973, pp. 99-105), Strauss (1987, Chapters 1, 5, and 6), and Strauss and Corbin (1990, Chapter 12).

5. See Mills (1959) for advice on how to use memos in developing a research agenda and career.

2

Purposes:
Why Are You Doing This Study?

In planning, as well as in assessing, ethnographic research, we must consider its relevance as well as its validity.

Hammersley, 1992, p. 85

It is relatively easy to find an unanswered, empirically answerable question to which the answer isn't *worth* knowing; as Thoreau said, it is not worthwhile to go around the world to count the cats in Zanzibar. In addition, it is easy to become captivated by the stories of your informants, or by what's going on in the setting you are studying, and lose sight of the *reasons* for studying these particular phenomena. Brendan Croskery (1995), reflecting on his dissertation research on four Newfoundland school principals, admitted that "the study suffered from too many good intentions and too little focused thinking. . . . I painfully discovered that many of the data (though interesting) were not particularly relevant to the core category" (p. 348).

Without a clear sense of the purposes behind your work, you are apt to lose your way or to spend your time and effort doing things that won't contribute to your goals in conducting the research.

Thus, the purposes of your study are an essential part of your research design. (I am using *purpose* in a broad sense to include motives, desires, and goals—anything that leads you to do the study or that you hope to accomplish by doing it.) These purposes serve two important functions. First, they help to guide your other design decisions to ensure that your study is worth doing, that you get out of it what you want. Second, they are crucial to *justifying* your study, a key task of your proposal.

PERSONAL, PRACTICAL,
AND RESEARCH PURPOSES

It is useful to distinguish between three different kinds of purposes for doing a study: personal purposes, practical purposes, and research purposes. Personal purposes are those that motivate *you* to do this study; they can include such things as a political passion to change some existing situation, a curiosity about a specific phenomenon or event, a desire to engage in a particular type of research, or simply the need to advance your career. These personal purposes often overlap with your practical or research purposes, but they may also include deeply rooted individual desires and needs that bear little relationship to the "official" reasons for doing the study.

One purpose in particular that deserves thought is your motivation for choosing a qualitative approach. Locke, Spirduso, and Silverman (1993) argue that "every graduate student who is tempted to employ a qualitative design should confront one question, 'Why do I want to do a qualitative study?' and then answer it honestly" (p. 107). They emphasize that qualitative research is *not* easier than quantitative and that seeking to avoid statistics bears little relationship to having the personal interests and skills that qualitative inquiry requires (pp. 107-110). The key issue is the compatibility of your reasons for "going qualitative" with your other purposes, your research questions, and the requirements for carrying out a qualitative study.

Traditionally, discussions of research design have been based, implicitly or explicitly, on the positivist ideal of the objective and disinterested scientist, emphasizing that the choice of research approaches and methods should be determined by the research questions that you want to answer. However, it is clear from autobiographies of scientists that research decisions are often far more personal than this, and the importance of subjective motives and goals in science is supported by a great deal of historical, sociological, and philosophical work.

The grain of truth in the traditional view is that your personal (and often unexamined) motives as researcher have important consequences for the validity of your conclusions. If your design decisions and data analyses are based on personal desires *without* a careful assessment of the implications of these for your methods and conclusions, you are in danger of creating a flawed study. King Gustav of Sweden wanted a powerful warship to dominate the Baltic, but this desire led to an ill-considered decision to add a second gundeck to the *Vasa*, causing it to capsize and sink and thus dealing a severe setback to his purposes.

For this reason, it is important that you recognize and take account of the personal purposes that drive and inform your research. Attempting to purge yourself of personal goals and concerns is neither possible nor necessary. What *is* necessary is to be aware of these concerns and how they may be shaping your research, and to think about how best to deal with their consequences. In addition, recognizing your personal ties to the study you want to conduct can provide you with a valuable source of insight, theory, and data about the phenomena you are studying (Marshall & Rossman, 1995, pp. 22-25; Strauss & Corbin, 1990, pp. 42-43); this source will be discussed in the next chapter, under the heading of Experiential Knowledge.

Identifying your purposes is not something you can do when you begin designing the study and then forget about. Some of these purposes may not become apparent to you until you are well into the research; in addition, they may change as the research proceeds. Example 2.1 describes how one researcher's purposes influenced and informed a series of qualitative studies.

Besides your personal purposes, there are two other, more public kinds of purposes that I want to distinguish and discuss: practical purposes (including administrative or policy purposes) and research purposes. Practical purposes are focused on *accomplishing* something—meeting some need, changing some situation, or achieving some goal. Research purposes, on the other hand, are focused on *understanding* something, gaining some insight into what is going on and why this is happening.

Both of these kinds of purposes are legitimate parts of your design. However, they need to be distinguished, because although research purposes are often a fruitful starting point for framing research questions, practical purposes can rarely be used in this straightforward way. Research questions need to be empirically answerable by your study, and questions of the form "How can this program be improved?" or "What is the best way to increase students' understanding of science?" are not directly answerable by any empirical research. Such questions have an inherent value component that no amount of data can directly address. On the other hand, research questions such as "What effect has this change had on the program?" or "What were the consequences of these teaching methods for students' understanding of science?" not only are potentially answerable, but they directly contribute to the practical purposes implied in the previous questions.

For these reasons, you need to frame your research questions in ways that help your study to advance your purposes, rather than smuggling these purposes into the research questions themselves, where they may play havoc with the coherence and feasibility of your design. I will discuss this issue more fully in Chapter 4 on research questions; here, I am simply emphasizing that the two need to be kept distinct.

To repeat, I am not telling you to eliminate practical purposes from your design. Practical or political ends can be a legitimate part of your purposes; your intent should not be to eradicate these but to understand where they are coming from and what their implications are for your research.

THE STRENGTHS OF
QUALITATIVE RESEARCH

Qualitative and quantitative methods are not simply different ways of doing the same thing. Instead, they have different strengths and logics and are often best used to address different questions and purposes.[1] The strengths of qualitative research derive primarily from its inductive approach, its focus on specific situations or people, and its emphasis on words rather than numbers.

There are five particular *research* purposes for which qualitative studies are especially suited:

1. Understanding the *meaning,* for participants in the study, of the events, situations, and actions they are involved with and of the accounts that they give of their lives and experiences. I am using "meaning" here in a broad sense to include cognition, affect, intentions, and anything else that can be included in what qualitative researchers often refer to as the "participants' perspective. " The perspective on events and actions held by the people involved in them is not simply their account of these events and actions, to be assessed in terms of its truth or falsity; it is *part of* the reality that you are trying to understand (Maxwell, 1992; Menzel, 1978). In a qualitative study, you are interested not only in the physical events and behavior that is taking place, but also in how the participants in your study make sense of this and how their understandings influence their behavior. This focus on meaning is central to what is known as the "interpretive" approach to social science (Bredo & Feinberg, 1982; Geertz, 1973; Rabinow & Sullivan, 1979).

2. Understanding the particular *context* within which the participants act, and the influence that this context has on their actions. Qualitative researchers typically study a relatively small number of individuals or

---

EXAMPLE 2.1
The Importance of Personal Values and Identity

Alan Peshkin's personal purposes, rooted in his own values and identity, have profoundly influenced several ethnographic studies he has done of schools and their communities (Glesne & Peshkin, 1992, pp. 93-107; Peshkin, 1991, pp. 285-295). In his first study, in a rural town he called Mansfield, he liked the community and felt protective toward it. This shaped the kind of story that he told, a story about the importance of community and its preservation. In contrast, in his second study, an ethnography of a fundamentalist Christian school (which he called Bethany Baptist Academy) and its community, he felt alienated, as a Jew, from a community that attempted to proselytize him:

> When I began to write . . . I knew I was annoyed by my *personal* (as opposed to research) experience at BBA. I soon became sharply aware that my annoyance was pervasively present, that I was writing out of pique and vexation. Accordingly, I was not celebrating community at Bethany, and community prevailed there no less robustly than it had at Mansfield. Why not? I was more than annoyed in Bethany; my ox had been gored. The consequence was that the story I was feeling drawn to tell had its origins in my personal sense of threat. I was not at Bethany as a cool, dispassionate observer (are there any?); I was there as a Jew whose otherness was dramatized directly and indirectly during 18 months of fieldwork. (Glesne & Peshkin, 1992, p. 103)

In hindsight, Peshkin realized that if he had been less sympathetic toward Mansfield, he could have told a different, equally valid story about this community, whereas if he had identified with Bethany and wanted to support and perpetuate it, he could legitimately have showed how it was much like Mansfield.

In a third study, this one of an urban, multiethnic and multiracial school and community that he called Riverview, Peshkin resolved at the outset to try to identify the aspects of his identity that he saw emerging in his reactions. He lists six different subjective *I's* that influenced this study, each embodying its own purposes. These included the Ethnic-Maintenance *I* and the Community-Maintenance *I* that he had discovered in his earlier studies; an E-Pluribus-Unum *I* that supported the ethnic and racial mingling that he saw going on; a Justice-Seeking *I* that wanted to correct the negative and biased images of Riverview held by its wealthier neighbors; a Pedagogical-Meliorist *I* that was disturbed by the poor teaching that many minority students received in Riverview and sought to find ways to improve this; and a Nonresearch-Human *I* that was grateful for the warm reception he and his wife received in Riverview, generated a concern for the people and community, and moderated otherwise sharp judgments he might have made.

In addition to influencing his questions and conclusions, Peshkin's personal purposes were intimately involved in his choice of methods. He states that

> I like fieldwork, it suits me, and I concluded that rather than pursuing research with questions in search of the "right" methods of data collection, I had a preferred method of data collection in search of the "right" question. (Glesne & Peshkin, 1992, p. 102)

Peshkin strongly recommends that all researchers systematically monitor their subjectivity:

> I see this monitoring as a necessary exercise, a workout, a tuning up of my subjectivity to get it in shape. It is a rehearsal for keeping the lines of my subjectivity open—and straight. And it is a warning to myself so that I may avoid the trap of perceiving just what my own untamed sentiments have sought out and served up as data. (Peshkin, 1991, pp. 293-294)

Exercise 2.1 is one way to engage in this monitoring.

---

situations and preserve the individuality of each of these in their analyses, rather than collecting data from large samples and aggregating the data across individuals or situations. Thus, they are able to understand how events, actions, and meanings are shaped by the unique circumstances in which these occur.

3. Identifying *unanticipated* phenomena and influences, and generating new grounded theories about the latter. Qualitative research has long been used for this purpose by survey and experimental researchers, who often conduct exploratory qualitative studies to help them design their questionnaires and identify variables for experimental investigation. Although qualitative research is not restricted to this exploratory role, it is still an important strength of qualitative methods.

4. Understanding the *process* by which events and actions take place. Merriam (1988) states that "the interest [in a qualitative study] is in process rather than outcomes" (p. xii); although this does not mean that qualitative research is unconcerned with outcomes, it does emphasize that a major

strength of qualitative research is in getting at the processes that led to these outcomes, processes that experimental and survey research are often poor at identifying (Britan, 1978; Patton, 1990, p. 94ff.).

5. Developing *causal explanations*. The traditional view that qualitative research cannot identify causal relationships has long been disputed by some qualitative researchers (Britan, 1978; Denzin, 1970), and it is being increasingly abandoned by both qualitative and quantitative researchers (Cook & Shadish, 1985; Erickson, 1986/1990, p. 82; Miles & Huberman, 1994, pp. 144-148; Robson, 1993, p. 42; Rossi & Berk, 1991, p. 226; Sayer, 1992). Miles and Huberman (1984) earlier argued that

> much recent research supports a claim that we wish to make here: that field research is far *better* than solely quantified approaches at developing explanations of what we call local causality—the actual events and processes that led to specific outcomes. (p. 132)

Part of the reason for the disagreement has been a failure to recognize that quantitative and qualitative researchers tend to ask different kinds of causal questions. Quantitative researchers tend to be interested in whether and to what extent variance in x causes variance in y. Qualitative researchers, on the other hand, tend to ask *how* x plays a role in causing y, what the process is that connects x and y.[2] Mohr (1982) has defined this as the distinction between variance theory and process theory; Ragin (1987) makes a similar distinction between variable-oriented and case-oriented methods. Variance theory deals with variables and the correlations among them; it is based on an analysis of the contribution of differences in values of particular variables to differences in other variables. Process theory, in contrast, deals with events and the processes that connect them; it is based on an analysis of the causal processes by which some events influence others. Britan (1978) argues that

> experimental evaluations relate program treatments to program effects without directly examining causal processes, [while] contextual evaluations investigate causal relationships . . . by directly examining the processes through which results are achieved. (p. 231)

Weiss (1994) provides a concrete example of this difference:

> In qualitative interview studies the demonstration of causation rests heavily on the description of a visualizable sequence of events, each event flowing into the next. . . . Quantitative studies support an assertion of

causation by showing a correlation between an earlier event and a subsequent event. An analysis of data collected in a large-scale sample survey might, for example, show that there is a correlation between the level of the wife's education and the presence of a companionable marriage. In qualitative studies, we would look for a process through which the wife's education or factors associated with her education express themselves in marital interaction. (p. 179)

This is not to say that deriving causal explanations from a qualitative study is an easy or straightforward task. However, the situation of qualitative research is no different from quantitative research in this respect. Both approaches need to identify and deal with the plausible validity threats to any proposed causal explanation, as discussed in Chapter 6.

These research purposes, and the inductive, open-ended strategy that they require, give qualitative research an advantage in addressing three *practical* purposes:

1. Generating results and theories that are understandable and experientially credible, both to the people you are studying and to others. Patton (1990, pp. 19-24) gives an example of how the open-ended responses to a questionnaire used to evaluate a teacher accountability system had far greater credibility with, and impact on, the school administration than did the quantitative analysis of the standardized items. Bolster (1983) makes a more general argument, that one of the reasons for the lack of impact of educational research on educational practice has been that such research has largely been quantitative and doesn't connect with teachers' experience of everyday classroom realities. He argues for a qualitative approach that emphasizes the perspective of teachers and the understanding of particular settings, as having far more potential for informing educational practitioners.

2. Conducting formative evaluations, ones that are intended to help improve existing practice rather than to simply assess the value of the program or product being evaluated (Scriven, 1967, 1991). In such evaluations, it is more important to understand the process by which things happen in a particular situation than to rigorously compare this with other situations.

3. Engaging in collaborative or action research with practitioners or research participants. The face credibility of qualitative research, as well as its focus on particular contexts and their meaning for the participants in these contexts, makes it particularly suitable for collaborations with these participants (Bolster, 1983; Patton, 1990, pp. 129-130; Reason, 1988,

EXAMPLE 2.2
Deciding on a Dissertation Topic

During her first year of doctoral work, Isabel Londoño, a native of Colombia, enrolled in a qualitative research methods course. For her research project, she interviewed seven women from her country who were working in Boston, exploring their experiences balancing work and family. While working on the project, she also began to read some of the feminist literature available in the United States on women executives, women's psychological development, and women's experience managing work and family. She was excited by the new ideas in this literature, which she had not had access to in her own country, and decided that she wanted to focus on issues of executive women in her country for her dissertation.

At the end of her first year, Isabel took a leave of absence from the doctoral program to work as the chief of staff to her former college roommate, whose husband had just been elected president of Columbia. Among her responsibilities was gathering information on employment, education, and the status of women in her nation. One of the issues that emerged as critical was the need to assess the effect of a recent shift in educational decision making from the national to the local level. In the past, most decisions had been made by the national ministry of education; now decisions were being shifted downward to the mayors in local municipalities. No one was really sure how this change was being implemented and what its effects were.

Isabel found that investigating an issue that affected the lives of many people in her country changed her perspective, and raised questions about her choice of a thesis topic:

> It became an issue of what was my responsibility to the world. To find out how to solve a personal, internal conflict of executive women? Or was there a problem where I could really be of help? Also, what was more rewarding to me as a person—to solve a problem that affected me personally or solve a problem of the world?

She also felt pressure from others to select a topic that clearly linked to her career goals and showed that she knew what she wanted to do with her life.

Coming to a decision about her dissertation research topic forced Isabel to identify and assess her personal and practical purposes.

> I thought about why I got into a doctoral program. What I hoped to get out of it personally, professionally, academically. Why did I end

up here? Then, I thought about what are the things about the world that move me, that make me sad or happy? I analyzed what that interest was about—people, feelings, institutions. It was important for me to see the themes in common in my interests and motivations. It gave me strength. I also was open to change. Change is the most scary thing, but you have to allow it.

She decided that she would study the decentralization of educational decision making in six municipalities in her country. In making this decision, she chose to disregard others' opinions of her:

What I have decided is *no,* I am going to do my thesis about something that *moves me inside.* I don't care if I am ever going to work on that topic again because it's something I want to learn about. I don't want to use my thesis as a stepladder for my work, that feels like prostitution. So I believe the interest should be on the thesis topic itself, not on where that is leading you, where you're going to get with it.

One of the things that supported her decision was reading the literature on her topic:

That was very important because I discovered that what I was interested in was something that had interested a lot of other people before, and was going on in a lot of other places in the world, and was affecting education in other countries. This made my topic relevant. It was very important for me to understand that it was relevant, that I was not just making up a dream problem. I think that's something you always fear, that the problem you see is not really important. I also learned that although other people had done work on the problem, *nobody* had the interest I had—the human impact of implementing a reform in the administration of education.
Writing memos for classes was key, having to put things to paper. I also started keeping a thesis diary and wrote memos to myself in it. The date and one word, one idea, or something that I'd read. Many of the things I've written about have now become the list of what I'm going to do *after* I do my thesis!
Finally, I think it's important to really try to have fun. I figure, if you don't have fun you shouldn't be doing it. Of course, sometimes I get tired of my topic and hate it. I sit at the computer and I'm tired and I don't want to do it, but every time I start working I forget all that and get immersed in my work. And if something has the power to do that, it must be right.

1994). In addition, there are important ethical reasons for incorporating the perspectives and purposes of these participants (Lincoln, 1990).

Sorting out and assessing the different personal, practical, and research purposes that you bring to your study can be a difficult task, as Peshkin indicates. Example 2.2 provides an account of how one doctoral student, Isabel Londoño, went about identifying her purposes in making a decision about her dissertation topic. As Isabel describes it, memo writing can be very helpful in this process, and Exercise 2.1 gives you an opportunity to begin doing this for your own study.

EXERCISE 2.1
Reflecting on Your Purposes

Write a memo on why you want to do the study you are designing. What personal and practical purposes, as well as research purposes, are involved in this research? Think about the different *I's* that may come into play in your study, and what the values and goals of these different *I's* are. Finally, try to identify the implications of each of these identities and purposes for the rest of your design. What do they suggest about the kinds of questions you should try to answer, the theories that are relevant to these, the setting or population you need to study, the kinds of methods you should use, or potential validity threats to your conclusions that you will need to deal with?

NOTES

1. I've developed this distinction in more detail in an unpublished paper (Maxwell, 1996b). See also Patton (1990, pp. 92-141) and Robson (1993, pp. 38-45).

2. This is only a tendency, not an absolute difference between the two. For an approach to qualitative design that is based primarily on variance theory, see King, Keohane, and Verba (1994).

3

Conceptual Context:
What Do You Think Is Going On?

Biologist Bernd Heinrich (1984, pp. 141-151) and his associates once spent a summer conducting detailed, systematic research on ant lions, small insects that trap ants in pits they have dug. Returning to the university in the fall, Heinrich was surprised to discover that his results were quite different from those published by other researchers. Redoing his experiments the following summer to try to understand these discrepancies, Heinrich found that he and his fellow researchers had been led astray by an unexamined assumption they had made about the ant lions' time frame: their observations hadn't been long enough to detect some key aspects of these insects' behavior. He concluded that "even carefully collected results can be misleading if the underlying context of assumptions is wrong" (p. 151).

For this reason, the conceptual context of your study—the system of concepts, assumptions, expectations, beliefs, and theories that supports and informs your research—is a key part of your design. This context, or a diagrammatic representation of it, is often called a *conceptual framework* (Miles & Huberman, 1994; Robson, 1993). Miles and Huberman (1994) state that a conceptual framework "explains, either graphically or in narrative form, the main things to be studied—the key factors, concepts, or variables—and the presumed relationships among them" (p. 18).

The most important thing to understand about your conceptual context is that it is a formulation of what you think is *going on* with the phenomena you are studying—a tentative *theory* of what is happening and why. The function of this theory is to inform the rest of your design—to help you to assess your purposes, develop and select realistic and relevant research questions and methods, and identify potential validity threats to your conclusions. In this chapter, I discuss the different sources for this theory. I describe the nature of theory in more detail later in the chapter, in dealing with the uses of existing theory; here, I want to emphasize that your conceptual context *is* a theory, what is sometimes called the *theoretical framework* for the study.

Some writers label this part of a research design or proposal the *literature review.* This can be a dangerously misleading term. In constructing this part of your design, you should *not* simply summarize some body of empirical or theoretical publications, for three reasons:

1. It can lead to a narrow focus on literature, ignoring other conceptual resources that may be of equal or greater importance for your study. Locke et al. (1993) point out that "in any active area of inquiry, the current knowledge base is not in the library—it is in the invisible college of informal associations among research workers" (p. 48). This knowledge can be found in unpublished papers, dissertations in progress, and grant applications, as well as in the heads of researchers working in this field. Locke et al. (1993) state that "the best introduction to the current status of a research area is close association with advisers who know the territory" (p. 49). In addition, an exclusive orientation toward the literature leads you to ignore your own experience, your speculative thinking (discussed below under Thought Experiments), and your pilot and exploratory research.

2. It tends to generate a strategy of covering the field rather than focusing specifically on those studies and theories that are particularly relevant to your research. Literature reviews that lose sight of this need for relevance often degenerate into a series of "book reports" on the literature, with no clear connecting thread or argument. The relevant studies may only be a small subset of the research in a defined field, and they may range across a number of different disciplines and approaches. In fact, the most productive ways of constructing a conceptual context are often those that integrate different approaches, lines of investigation, or theories that no one had previously connected. Bernd Heinrich used Adam Smith's *The Wealth of Nations* in developing a theory of bumblebee foraging and energy balance that emphasized individual initiative, competition, and a spontaneous division of labor, rather than genetic determination or centralized control (Heinrich, 1979, pp. 144-146; 1984, pp. 79ff.).

3. It can make you think that your task is simply descriptive—to tell what previous researchers have found or what theories have been proposed. In constructing a conceptual context, your purpose is not only descriptive, but also critical; you need to understand (and clearly communicate in your proposal) what the *problems* (including ethical problems) have been with previous research and theory, what contradictions or holes you have found in existing views, and how your study can make an original contribution to our understanding. (For an example of this, see the Context section of Martha Regan-Smith's proposal, in Appendix A.) You need to treat the literature not

as an *authority* to be deferred to, but as a useful but fallible source of *ideas* about what's going on, and you should attempt to see alternative ways of framing the issues. Heinrich found that many of the ideas about ant lions in the literature were wrong, and his subsequent research led to a much more comprehensive and well-supported theory of their behavior.

Another way of putting this is that the conceptual context for your research study is something that is *constructed,* not found. It incorporates pieces that are borrowed from elsewhere, but the structure, the overall coherence, is something that *you* build, not something that exists ready-made. It is important for you to pay attention to the existing theories and research that are relevant to what you plan to study, because these are often key sources for understanding what is going on with these phenomena. However, these theories and results are sometimes misleading or flawed, and you will need to critically examine each piece of existing material to see if it is a valid and useful module for constructing the theory that will best inform your study.[1]

There are four main sources for the modules that you can use to construct the conceptual context for your study: your own experiential knowledge, existing theory and research, pilot and exploratory research, and thought experiments. I will begin with experiential knowledge, both because it is one of the most important conceptual resources, and because it is the one that is most seriously neglected in works on research design. I will then deal with the use of existing theory and research in research design, in the process introducing a tool, known as *concept mapping,* which can be valuable in formulating a tentative theory, or conceptual framework, for the study you are designing. Finally, I will discuss the value of your own pilot research and thought experiments in developing a conceptual context for your research.

EXPERIENTIAL KNOWLEDGE

Traditionally, what you bring to the research from your background and identity has been treated as *bias,* something whose influence needs to be eliminated from the design, rather than a valuable component of it. This has been true to some extent even in qualitative research, where it has long been recognized that the researcher *is* the instrument of the research. In opposition to this view, C. Wright Mills (1959), in a classic essay, argues that "the most admirable scholars within the scholarly community . . . do not split their work from their lives. They seem to take both too seriously to allow such dissociation, and they want to use each for the enrichment of the other" (p. 195).

Separating your research from other aspects of your life cuts you off from a major source of insights, hypotheses, and validity checks. Alan Peshkin, discussing the role of subjectivity in the research he has done, concludes that

> the subjectivity that originally I had taken as an affliction, something to bear because it could not be foregone, could, to the contrary, be taken as "virtuous." My subjectivity is *the* basis for the story that I am able to tell. It is a strength on which I build. It makes me who I am as a person *and* as a researcher, equipping me with the perspectives and insights that shape all that I do as a researcher, from the selection of topics clear through to the emphases I make in my writing. Seen as virtuous, subjectivity is something to capitalize on rather than to exorcise. (Glesne & Peshkin, 1992, p. 104)

Anselm Strauss (1987) emphasizes many of the same points in discussing what he calls *experiential data*—the researcher's technical knowledge, research background, and personal experiences. He argues that

> these experiential data should not be ignored because of the usual canons governing research (which regard personal experience and data as likely to bias the research), for these canons lead to the squashing of valuable experiential data. We say, rather, "mine your experience, there is potential gold there!" (p. 11)

Students' proposals often seem to systematically ignore what their authors know from their own experience about the settings or issues they propose to study; this can seriously damage the proposal's credibility.

Both Peshkin and Strauss emphasize that this is not a license to uncritically impose one's assumptions and values on the research. Reason (1988, 1994) uses the term *critical subjectivity* to refer to

> a quality of awareness in which we do not suppress our primary experience; nor do we allow ourselves to be swept away and overwhelmed by it; rather we raise it to consciousness and use it as part of the inquiry process. (1988, p. 12)

The explicit incorporation of your identity and experience in your research has recently gained much wider theoretical and philosophical support (e.g., Berg & Smith, 1988; Jansen & Peshkin, 1992). The philosopher Hilary Putnam (1987, 1990) argues that there cannot, even in principle, be such a thing as a "God's eye view," a view that is the one true objective account. *Any* view is a view from *some perspective,* and therefore incorporates the stance of the observer.

Philosophical argument does not, however, solve the problem of how to assess the effect of your experience on the research or how to incorporate this experience most productively in your research design. Peshkin's account of how he became aware of the different *I's* that influenced and informed his studies was discussed in Chapter 2, and Jansen and Peshkin (1992) and Grady and Wallston (1988, pp. 40-43) provide valuable examples of researchers using their own subjectivity and experience in their research. At present, however, there are few well-developed and explicit strategies for doing this.

One technique that I use for this is an exercise that I call a *researcher experience memo* (see Exercise 3.1). I originally got the idea for this from a talk by Robert Bogdan, who described how, before beginning a study of a hospital's neonatal intensive care unit, he tried to write out all of the expectations, beliefs, and assumptions that he had about hospitals in general and neonatal care in particular, as a way of identifying and taking account of the perspective that he brought to the study. This exercise can be valuable at any point in a study, not just at the outset. Example 3.1 is part of one of my own experience memos, written while I was working on a theoretical paper on diversity, solidarity, and community (Maxwell, 1996a). Grady and Wallston (1988, p. 41) provide a memo in which the researcher used her own experience to design a study of why many women don't do breast self-examination.

EXISTING THEORY AND RESEARCH

The second major source of modules for your conceptual context is existing theory and research—not simply published work but other people's theories and empirical research as a whole. I will begin with theory, because it is for most people the more problematic and confusing of the two, and then deal with using existing research for other purposes than as a source of theory.

I'm using the term *theory* to refer to something that is considerably broader than the usual meaning in discussions of research methods. By theory, I mean simply a set of concepts and the proposed relationships

EXAMPLE 3.1
Experience Memo on Diversity

I can't recall when I first became interested in diversity; it's been a major concern for at least the last 20 years. . . . I do remember the moment that I consciously realized that my mission in life was "to make the world safe for diversity"; I was in Regenstein library at the University of Chicago one night in the mid-70s talking to another student about why we had gone into anthropology, and the phrase suddenly popped into my head.

However, I never gave much thought to tracing this position any further back. I remember, as an undergraduate, attending a talk on some political topic and being struck by two students' bringing up issues of the rights of particular groups to retain their cultural heritages; it was an issue that had never consciously occurred to me. And I'm sure that my misspent youth reading science fiction rather than studying had a powerful influence on my sense of the importance of tolerance and understanding of diversity; I wrote my essay for my application to Reed College on tolerance in high school society. But I didn't think much about where all this came from.

It was talking to the philosopher Amelie Rorty in the summer of 1991 that really triggered my awareness of these roots. She had given a talk on the concept of moral diversity in Plato, and I gave her a copy of my draft paper on diversity and solidarity. We met for lunch several weeks later to discuss these issues, and at one point, she asked me how my concern with diversity connected with my background and experiences. I was surprised by the question and found I really couldn't answer it. She, on the other hand, had thought about this a lot, and talked about her parents emigrating from Belgium to the United States, deciding they were going to be farmers like "real Americans," and with no background in farming, buying land in rural West Virginia and learning how to survive and fit into a community composed of people very different from themselves.

This made me start thinking, and I realized that as far back as I can remember I've felt different from other people, and had a lot of difficulties as a result of this difference and my inability to "fit in" with peers, relatives, or other people generally. This was all compounded by my own shyness and tendency to isolate myself, and by the frequent moves that my family made while I was growing up. . . .

The way in which this connects with my work on diversity is that my main strategy for dealing with my difference from others, as far back as I can remember, was *not* to try to be more *like* them (similarity-based), but to try to be *helpful* to them (contiguity-based). This is a bit oversimplified, because I also saw myself as somewhat of a "social chameleon," adapting to whatever situation I was in, but this adaptation was much more

> an *interactional* adaptation than one of becoming fundamentally similar to other people.
>
> It now seems incomprehensible to me that I never saw the connections between this background and my academic work. . . . [The remainder of the memo discusses the specific connections between my experience and the theory of diversity and community that I had been developing, which sees both similarity (shared characteristics) and contiguity (interaction) as possible sources of solidarity (Maxwell, 1996a).]

among these, a structure that is intended to represent or model something about the world. LeCompte and Preissle (1993) state that "theorizing is simply the cognitive process of discovering or manipulating abstract categories and the relationships among these categories" (p. 239). My only modification of this is to include not simply abstract categories but concrete and specific concepts as well.

This use encompasses everything from so-called "grand theory," such as postmodernism, psychoanalysis, or rational choice theory, to specific, everyday explanations of a particular event or characteristic, such as "Jim was late for class because his car had a flat tire." That is, I'm not using "theory" to denote a particular level of complexity, abstraction, or generality of explanatory propositions, but to refer to the *entire range* of such propositions. All such explanations have fundamental features in common, and, for my purposes, the similarities are more important than the differences.[2]

One of my goals in doing this is to demystify the concept of theory, so that, like the character in Moliere's play, *Le Bourgeois Gentilhomme,* who was delighted to discover that all his life he had been speaking prose, you will realize that all your life you have been creating and using theory. Theory is not an arcane and mysterious entity that at some point in your training you learn to understand and master; as Groucho Marx used to say on the 1950s TV game show *You Bet Your Life,* "It's an ordinary household word, something you use every day."

The simplest form of theory is what I call a "barbell theory." This consists of two concepts joined by a proposed relationship (see Figure 3.1). Such a theory can be as general as "positive reinforcement leads to continuation of the reinforced behavior," or as specific as "Nixon was able to establish relations with China because he was trusted by conservatives." The important point is what *makes* this a theory: the linking of two concepts by a proposed relationship.

Figure 3.1. A Simple Theory

   Having presented this broad conception of theory, however, I want to qualify it somewhat by distinguishing theory from two things that could also fit this model, but which I think are better distinguished from theory proper. These are what I have elsewhere (Maxwell, 1992) called description and interpretation. *Description* is simply a factual narrative of what happened, at a very low level of abstraction. It is not theory because the connections between the events are neither abstract nor explanatory, but simply spatial and chronological; it makes no attempt to go beyond what is immediately or potentially observable. For example, a description of what happened in a particular meeting would include a detailed account of the physical aspects of the setting, the actions of the people, and the words they spoke, but it would not go beyond this to propose an explanation of what was going on, or to fit this into a more abstract framework.

   Interpretation, as I use the term, also differs from theory. It refers to an account of the meaning given to some situation or event by the people studied, in their own terms (see the discussion of meaning in Chapter 2). Interpretation, in this sense, is not theory for the same reason that description is not theory: it is simply a concrete account of that meaning and has no explanatory intent. An interpretation of the previously mentioned meeting would attempt to infer the meaning that the setting, actions, and words had for the people in this meeting, but it would not attempt to explain that meaning or fit it into a more abstract framework.

   To take either description or interpretation and construct an explanation based on these, or to fit them into an existing explanatory framework, is to convert them into theory. Of course, all description and interpretation are inherently theory-laden, rather than being pure, objective accounts of events or meanings. But unless the intent is to go beyond a concrete descriptive or interpretive account, the main purpose of theory, explanation, is not achieved.

   Thus, theory provides a model or map of *why* the world is the way it is (Strauss, 1995). It is a simplification of the world, but a simplification aimed at clarifying and explaining some aspect of how it works. Theory is a statement about what is going on with the phenomena that you want to understand. It is not simply a framework, although it can provide that; rather it is a *story* about what you think is happening and why. A useful theory is one that tells an enlightening story about some phenomenon, one that gives you new insights and broadens your understanding of that phenomenon.

Glaser and Strauss's (1967) term *grounded theory* does not refer to any particular level of theory but to theory that is inductively developed during a study (or series of studies) and in constant interaction with the data from that study. This theory is grounded in the actual data collected, in contrast to a theory that is developed conceptually and then simply tested against empirical data. In qualitative research, both existing theory and grounded theory are legitimate and valuable.

The Uses of Existing Theory

Using existing theory in qualitative research has both advantages and dangers, as discussed earlier. The advantages of existing theory can be illustrated by a number of metaphors:

Theory as Coat Closet. (I got this metaphor from Jane Margolis [personal communication], who once described Marxism as a coat closet: "You can hang anything in it.") A useful high-level theory gives you a framework for making sense of what you see. Particular pieces of data that otherwise might seem unconnected or irrelevant to one another or to your research questions can be related by fitting them into the theory. The concepts of the existing theory are the "coat hooks" in the closet; they provide places to "hang" data, showing their relationship to other data. However, no theory will accommodate all data equally well; a theory that neatly organizes some data will leave other data disheveled and lying on the floor, with no place to hang them.

Theory as Spotlight. A useful theory *illuminates* what you are seeing in your research. It draws your attention to particular events or phenomena and sheds light on relationships that might otherwise go unnoticed or be misunderstood. Bernd Heinrich (1984), discussing an incident in his investigation of caterpillars' feeding habits, states that

> the clipped leaf stood out as if flagged in red, because it didn't fit my expectations or theories about how I thought things ought to be. My immediate feeling was one of wonder. But the wonder was actually a composite of different theories that crowded my mind and vied with each other for validation or rejection. . . . Had I no theories at all, the partially eaten leaf on the ground would not have been noticed. (pp. 133-134)

By the same token, a theory that brightly illuminates one area will leave other areas in darkness; no theory can illuminate everything. A study that makes brilliant use of existing theory is described in Example 3.2.

However, Becker (1986) warns that the existing literature, and the assumptions embedded in it, can deform the way you frame your research, causing you to overlook important ways of conceptualizing your study or key implications of your results. The literature has the advantage of what he calls *ideological hegemony,* so that it is difficult to see any phenomena in ways that are different from those that are prevalent in the literature. Trying to fit your insights into this established framework can deform your argument, weakening its logic and making it harder for you to see what this new way of framing the phenomena might contribute. Becker explains how his own research on marijuana use was deformed by existing theory:

> When I began studying marijuana use in 1951, the ideologically dominant question, the only one worth looking at, was "Why do people do a weird thing like that?" and the ideologically preferred way of answering it was to find a psychological trait or social attribute which differentiated people who did from people who didn't. . . . My eagerness to show that this literature (dominated by psychologists and criminologists) was wrong led me to ignore what my research was really about. I had blundered onto, and then proceeded to ignore, a much larger and more interesting question: how do people learn to define their own internal experiences? (pp. 147-148)

I had the same experience with my dissertation research on kinship in an Inuit community in northern Canada. At the time that I conducted the research, the literature on kinship in anthropology was dominated by a debate between two theories of the meaning of kinship, one holding that in all societies, kinship was fundamentally a matter of biological relationship, the other arguing that biology was only one possible meaning of kinship terms, another being social relatedness. I framed my dissertation (Maxwell, 1986) in terms of these two theories, arguing that my evidence mainly supported the second of these theories, although with significant modifications. It was only years later that I realized my research was really about the nature of relationship and solidarity in small, traditional communities—were these based on, and conceptualized in terms of, perceived similarity, in this case biological similarity, or social interaction (Maxwell, 1996a)? My research would have been much more productive if I had grasped this theoretical way of framing the study at the outset.

Becker (1986) argues that there is no way to be sure when the dominant approach is wrong or misleading or when your alternative is superior. What

---

EXAMPLE 3.2

Using Existing Theory

Eliot Freidson's (1975) book *Doctoring Together: A Study of Professional Social Control* is an account of his research in a medical group
practice, trying to understand how the physicians and administrators he
studied identified and dealt with violations of professional norms. In
conceptualizing what was going on in this practice, he used three broad
theories of the social organization and control of work. He refers to these
as the entrepreneurial or physician-merchant model, deriving from the
work of Adam Smith; the bureaucratic or physician-official model, deriving to a substantial extent from Max Weber; and the professional or
physician-craftsman model, which has been less clearly conceptualized
and identified than the others. He demonstrates how all three theories
clarify the day-to-day work of the group he studied, and he draws far-
ranging implications for public policy from his results.

Freidson (1975) also used existing theory in a more focused (and
daring) manner to illuminate the results of his research. He argues that the
social norms held by the physicians he studied allowed considerable
differences of opinion about both the technical standards of work performance and the best way to deal with patients. These norms "limited the
critical evaluation of colleagues' work and discouraged the expression of
criticism" (p. 241). However, the norms also strongly opposed any outside
control of the physicians' practice, defining physicians as the only ones
capable of judging medical work: "The professional was treated as an
individual free to follow his own judgment without constraint, so long as
his behavior was short of blatant or gross deficiencies in performance and
inconvenience to colleagues" (p. 241). Freidson continues:

> This is a very special kind of community that, structurally and
> normatively, parallels that described by Jesse R. Pitts as the "delin-
> quent community" of French schoolchildren in particular and French
> collectivities in general during the first half of the twentieth century
> . . . . Its norms and practice were such as to both draw all members
> together defensively against the outside world . . . and, internally,
> to allow each his freedom to act as he willed. (pp. 243-244)

He goes on to present striking similarities between the medical practice
he studied and the French peer group structure identified by Pitts. He coins
the phrase *professional delinquent community* to refer to professional
groups such as the one he describes, and he uses Pitts's theory to illuminate the process by which this sort of community develops and persists.

you can do is to try to identify the ideological component of the established approach and to see what happens when you abandon these assumptions. He claims that "a serious scholar ought routinely to inspect competing ways of talking about the same subject matter" and warns: "Use the literature, don't let it use you" (p. 149). An awareness of alternative sources of concepts and theories about the phenomena you are studying—including sources other than "the literature"—is an important counterweight to the ideological hegemony of existing theory and research.

There are thus two main ways in which qualitative researchers often fail to make good use of theory: by not using it enough and by relying too heavily on it. The first fails to explicitly apply or develop any analytic abstractions or theoretical framework for the study, thus missing the insights that only theory can provide. Every research design needs *some* theory of the phenomena you are studying, even if it is only a commonsense one, to guide the other design decisions you make. The second type of failure has the opposite problem: it *imposes* theory on the study, shoehorning questions, methods, and data into preconceived categories and preventing the researcher from seeing events and relationships that don't fit the theory. The imposition of dominant theories is also a serious ethical problem, not simply a scientific or practical one (Lincoln, 1990). To be genuinely qualitative research, a study must take account of the theories and perspectives of those studied, rather than relying entirely on established views or the researcher's own perspective.

The tension between these two dangers is an inescapable part of research, not a problem that can be solved by some technique or insight. A key strategy for dealing with this is embodied in the scientific method, as well as in interpretive approaches such as hermeneutics: develop theories and continually *test* them, looking for discrepant data and alternative ways (including the research participants' ways) of making sense of the data. Heinrich (1984) describes searching for crows' nests, in which you look through the trees for a dark spot against the sky, and then try to see a glimmer of light through it (real crows' nests are opaque): "It was like science: first you look for something, and then when you think you have it, you do your best to prove yourself wrong" (p. 28).

CONCEPT MAPS

For many students, the development or use of explicit theory is the most daunting part of a qualitative study. At this point, therefore, I want to introduce a tool for developing and clarifying theory, known as *concept mapping*. It was originally developed by Joseph Novak (Novak & Gowin, 1984), first as a way to understand how students learned science, and then as a tool for teaching science. A similar strategy, called a *conceptual framework,* is presented by Miles and Huberman (1994, pp. 18-22). Anselm Strauss (1987, pp. 170ff.) provides a third variation, which he calls an *integrative diagram.* These approaches have so much in common that I will present them as a single strategy, ignoring for the moment some important differences in the way they are used.

Figures 3.2 to 3.6 provide a variety of examples of concept maps; further examples can be found in Miles and Huberman (1994) and Strauss (1987, pp. 170ff.). A concept map, like the theory it represents, is a picture of the *territory* you want to study, not of the study itself. It is a visual display of your current working theory—a picture of what you think is going on with the phenomenon you're studying. It is not a specific part of either a research design or a proposal; rather, it is a tool for developing the conceptual context for your design—for generating theory, and seeing the implications of theory, for your study. And like a theory, a concept map consists of two things: concepts and the relationships among them. These are usually represented, respectively, as labeled circles or boxes and as arrows or lines connecting them.

There are two main uses for concept maps:

1. To pull together, and make visible, what your implicit theory actually is, or to clarify an existing theory
2. To develop theory. Like memos, concept maps are a way of "thinking on paper" (Howard & Barton, 1986); they can show you unexpected connections or identify holes or contradictions in your theory, and help you to figure out ways to resolve the latter.

Concept maps usually require considerable reworking in order to get them to the point where they're most helpful to you; don't expect to generate your final map on the first try. One useful way of developing a concept map is on a blackboard, where you can erase unsuccessful attempts, or pieces that don't seem to work well, and play with possible arrangements and connections. (The disadvantage of this is that it doesn't automatically create a "paper trail" of your attempts, which can help you to avoid repeating the same mistakes and to understand how your theory has changed.) There are also a variety of computer programs that can be used to create concept maps (Weitzman & Miles, 1995). Strauss (1987, pp. 171-182) provides a valuable transcript of his consultation with one

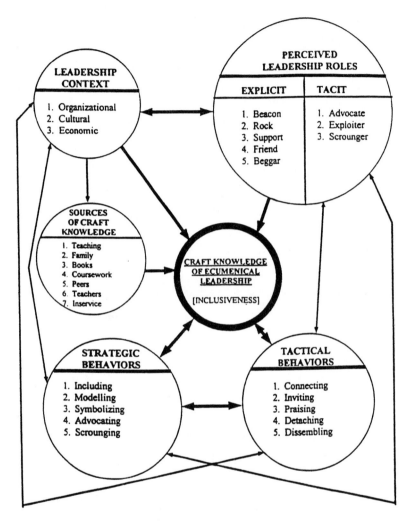

Figure 3.2. A Study of Newfoundland Principals' Craft Knowledge (Croskery, 1995)

student, Leigh Star, in helping her to develop a concept map for her research.

Avoid getting stuck in what Miles and Huberman (1994, p. 22) call a *no-risk map,* in which all the concepts are global and abstract and there are two-directional arrows everywhere. This sort of diagram can be useful as

(text continued on p. 41)

The following factors appear to influence the decision to keep at home an adult family member who is dependent because of disabilities, rather than "placing" or "institutionalizing" the adult child:

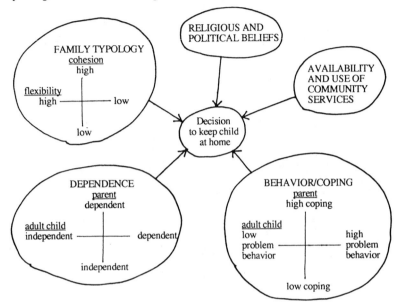

FAMILY TYPOLOGY is a model of intrafamily interactions and the permeability of family boundaries developed by David Kantor and expanded by Larry Constantine. Although I have not collected data on family typologies, intuition and existing data favor the prediction that families in the upper-right quadrant (*closed* family systems) and lower-right quadrant (*synchronous* family systems) are more likely to keep the dependent adult child at home, whereas families in the upper-left quadrant (*open* families) and lower- left quadrant (*random* families) are more likely to place the adult child.

In the Dependence grid, preliminary data indicate that the upper-left quadrant (high parental dependence, low child dependence) tends to correlate with a decision to keep the adult child at home, whereas the lower-right quadrant (parental independence, high care needs in child) tends to correlate with placing the adult child.

Similarly, in the Behavior/Coping grid, the upper-left quadrant (minimal behavior problems, high parental coping) tends to correlate with keeping the adult child at home, whereas the lower-right quadrant (serious behavior problems, low parental coping) tends to correlate with a decision to place the adult child.

Figure 3.3. Factors Affecting the Decision to Keep a Dependent Adult Child at Home (adapted from Guilbault, 1989)

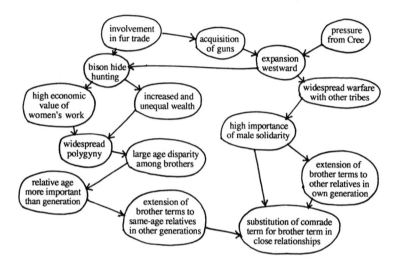

This map displays some of the events and influences leading to the widespread use of "brother" terms in Blackfeet society by the late 1800s. More than any other Plains tribe, the Blackfeet were involved in the fur trade. This led to increased wealth (including guns), a greater value of women's work in preparing bison hides for trade, a highly unequal distribution of wealth that favored men who had many horses for bison hunting, and a massive increase in polygyny, as wealthy men acquired large numbers of wives to process hides. The acquisition of guns and horses allowed the Blackfeet to move westward into the Plains, driving out the tribes that had previously lived there. The increase in warfare and bison hunting created a greater need for male solidarity and led to the widespread use of brother terms between men of the same generation to enhance this solidarity. However, the increased polygyny led to a wider range of ages within a man's generation and to the extension of brother terms to men of other generations who were of about the speaker's age. This proliferation of the use of brother terms eventually diluted their solidarity value, generating a new term, "comrade," which was often used in close relationships between men.

Figure 3.4. Causes of Changes in Blackfeet Kin Terminology (adapted from Maxwell, 1971, 1978)

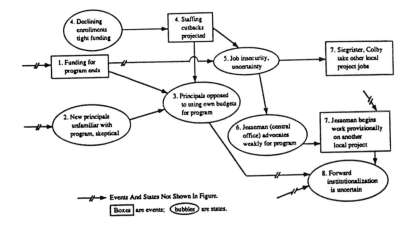

Figure 3.5. Excerpt From an Event-State Network: Perry-Parkdale School (Miles & Huberman, 1994)

a brainstorming exercise at the beginning, providing you with a conceptual checklist of things that may be important in your research, but at some point you need to focus the theory. It can be useful at some point to narrow your map to two concepts and the relationship between them, as a focusing exercise. Make commitments to what you think is most important and relevant in your theory.

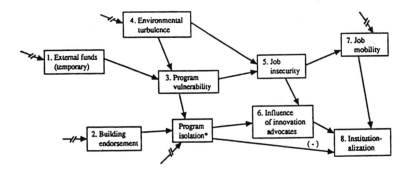

Figure 3.6. Excerpt From a Causal Network: Perry-Parkdale School (Miles & Huberman, 1994)

An initial framework often works best with large categories that hold a lot of things you haven't yet sorted out. However, you should try to differentiate these categories, making explicit your ideas about the relationships among the things in them. One way to start this is by analyzing each one into subcategories and identifying the different kinds of things that go into each. (Figure 3.2 does this for the peripheral categories that connect to the core category.) Another way is to *dimensionalize* the categories (Strauss & Corbin, 1990), trying to separate out their different properties (Figure 3.4 does this for several of the categories).

Beware of an elegant map; this may be the visual equivalent of what Becker (1986) calls "classy writing" (p. 28ff.), and it suggests that you may be emphasizing form at the expense of content. In particular, the presence of symmetry or duplication in a framework is a sign that you may be able to combine categories or restructure the relationships among the categories.

How do you know when something is a category or a relationship? This is not an easy question; I do this rather intuitively. In fact, many things can be seen as either; there is not one right concept map for the phenomena you're studying, and different maps incorporate different understandings of what's going on. You should try out alternative maps for the theory you are developing, rather than sticking rigidly with one formulation. There are also different *kinds* of concept maps, with different purposes; these include:

1. An abstract framework mapping the relationship among concepts
2. A flowchart-like account of events and how you think these are connected
3. A causal network of variables or influences
4. A treelike diagram of the meanings of words (e.g., Miles & Huberman, 1994, p. 133)
5. A Venn diagram, representing concepts as overlapping circles (e.g., Miles & Huberman, 1994, p. 249)

You can use more than one of these in a given study; the bottom line is its usefulness to you in advancing your understanding of what's going on. Most of Miles and Huberman's examples are best suited to studies of social processes; they aren't necessarily the most useful models for a study of meanings and their relationship to one another. Remember that a concept map is not an end in itself; it is a tool for developing theory and making that theory more explicit. Also, keep in mind that a concept map is not something that you do once and are finished with; you should go back and rework your concept maps as your understanding of the phenomena you are studying develops.

Different authors use concept maps in different ways. Novak and Gowin take a very diffuse approach—their concepts and relationships can be almost anything, and they label their connections in order to keep these clear. Miles and Huberman, on the other hand, are much more focused—their connections generally refer to causal relationships or influences. My advice is to aim for something in between. You can start with a fairly diffuse map, but you should work to focus it and to make it a map of a real theory of what's going on.

A key distinction, but one that you may not want to think about until after you've developed an initial concept map, is the difference between *variance* maps and *process* maps. One way to tell the difference is that a variance map usually deals with abstract, general concepts and is essentially timeless; it depicts how some factors or properties of things (conceptualized as variables) influence others. A process map, on the other hand, tells a chronological story; there is a beginning and end, and the categories are presented as specific events rather than variables.[3] Figures 3.3 and 3.6 are variance maps, whereas Figures 3.4 and 3.5 are process maps. Mixing variance and process approaches in a single map isn't impossible, but it can be difficult to do when you're just learning to use concept maps, and it can lead to confusion about the theory your map represents.

OTHER USES OF PRIOR RESEARCH

A review of relevant prior research can serve several other purposes in your design besides providing you with existing theory (cf. Strauss, 1987, pp. 48-56). First, it can be used to develop a justification for your study—to show how your work will address an important need or unanswered question (Marshall & Rossman, 1995, pp. 22-25); Martha Regan-Smith used prior research on medical school teaching in this way (Appendix A). Second, it can inform your decisions about methods, suggesting alternative approaches or revealing potential problems. Third, it can be a source of data that can be used to test or modify your theories. You can see if existing theory, pilot research, or your experiential understanding are supported or challenged by previous studies.

Finally, you can use prior research to help you generate theory. Bernd Heinrich (1984, pp. 55-68), in his thesis research on thermoregulation in sphinx moths, found that his experimental finding that these moths maintain a constant body temperature while flying was directly contradicted by others' research. He describes his response:

As a first step in my decision to proceed, I spent a few months in the library reading about insect physiology in general and everything about sphinx moths in particular. Something in the known physiology and morphology might provide a clue. It would be necessary to collect more and more details on the problem until I could visualize it as closely as if it were a rock sitting in the palm of my hand. I wanted to find out *how* the moths were thermoregulating. . . .

I came across an obscure French paper of 1919 by Franz Brocher on the anatomy of the blood circulatory system in sphinx moths. The odd thing about these moths is that the aorta makes a loop through their thoracic muscles. In many or most other insects, it passes *underneath* these muscles. (pp. 63-64)

This paper gave Heinrich the critical clue to how these moths were thermoregulating: they were shunting blood through the thoracic muscles to cool them and then losing the excess heat from the abdomen, in the same way that a car's water pump and radiator cool the engine. This theory was confirmed by subsequent experiments.

It is possible, of course, to become *too* immersed in the literature; as C. Wright Mills (1959) warns, "You may drown in it, like Mortimer Adler. Perhaps the point is to know when you ought to read, and when you ought not to" (p. 214). One of Mills's main ways of dealing with this problem was, in reading, to always be thinking of empirical studies that could test the ideas gained from the literature, both as preparation for actual research and as an exercise of the imagination (p. 205). These two strategies connect to the final two sources for your conceptual context: pilot studies and thought experiments.

PILOT AND EXPLORATORY STUDIES

Pilot studies serve some of the same functions as prior research, but they can be focused more precisely on your own concerns and theories. You can design pilot studies specifically to test your ideas or methods and explore their implications, or to inductively develop grounded theory. What Light, Singer, and Willett (1990) assert for an illustrative quantitative study is equally true for qualitative research: "Many features of their design could not be determined without prior exploratory research" (p. 212). And they argue that no design is ever so complete that it cannot be improved by a prior, small-scale exploratory study. Pilot studies are almost always worth the time and effort. Carry out a pilot study if *any* facet of your design needs clarification. (p. 213)

There is one particular use that pilot studies have in qualitative research, which prior research *can* also accomplish but is much less likely to. This use is to generate an understanding of the concepts and theories held by the people you are studying—what I have called interpretation (Maxwell, 1992). This is not simply a source of additional concepts for your theory, a type of concept that Strauss (1987, pp. 33-34) calls *in-vivo codes*. Instead, it provides you with an understanding of the meaning that these phenomena and events have for the actors who are involved in them, and the perspectives that inform their actions. In a qualitative study, these meanings and perspectives should constitute a key component of your theory; as discussed in Chapter 2, they are one of the things your theory is *about,* not simply a source of theoretical insights and building blocks for the latter.

THOUGHT EXPERIMENTS

Thought experiments have a long and respected tradition in the physical sciences (much of Einstein's work was based on thought experiments), but they have received little attention in discussions of research design, particularly qualitative research design. The best discussion of thought experiments in the social sciences that I know of is that of Lave and March (1975), who describe their book as "a practical guide to speculation." Asserting that "speculation is the soul of the social sciences" (p. 2), they provide a detailed introduction to the development and use of speculative models. Although the orientation of their later chapters is mainly quantitative, the earlier chapters are extremely useful for qualitative researchers.

Thought experiments draw on both theory and experience to answer "what if" questions, to seek out the logical implications of various properties of the phenomena you want to study. They can both test your current theory for logical problems and generate new theoretical insights. They encourage creativity and a sense of exploration, and they can help you to make explicit the experiential knowledge that you already possess. Finally, they are easy to do, once you develop the skill. Lave and March (1975) say,

We will treat models of human behavior as a form of art, and their development as a kind of studio exercise. Like all art, model building requires a combination of discipline and playfulness. It is an art that is learnable. It has explicit techniques, and practice leads to improvement. (p. 4)

For these techniques, I refer to you their presentation.

Experience, prior theory and research, pilot studies, and thought experiments are the four major sources of the conceptual context for your study. Putting together a conceptual context from these sources is a unique process for each study, and specific guidelines for how to do this are not of much use. The main thing to keep in mind is the need for integration of these components with one another, and with your purposes and research questions. The connections between your conceptual context and your research questions will be taken up in the next chapter.

EXERCISE 3.1
Reflecting on Your Experiential Context

This exercise is to write a memo on how your experience is relevant to your research. Use the memo to reflect on the context of what you bring to the study—your background, experiences, theoretical concepts, assumptions, values, and feelings. What prior connections do you have to the topics, issues, or settings you plan to investigate? How do these affect the way you are approaching your research? What is the lens through which you are looking at the phenomena you want to study?

This memo helps you to examine and critique these motives and assumptions and to discover what resources your experience provides. There is no particular structure that works best for the memo. However, you should *not* write a general account of your background and experiences; this is not an autobiography. You need to focus on those experiences, values, and assumptions that most directly relate to your planned research project and to reflect specifically on *how* these may affect your research.

This memo is for *your* benefit; try to avoid substituting presentation for reflection and analysis. I suggest beginning by brainstorming anything that comes to mind when you think about your site or topic and jotting these ideas down without immediately trying to organize or analyze them. One strategy that may be helpful in getting started on this memo is to "freewrite" responses to the following sentence-completion exercises; simply get your pen (or computer) moving and write whatever comes into your head in response to each of these, without trying to think carefully about your response, and then go on to the next one after a couple of minutes.

1. The thing I am most excited about in my study is . . .
2. My main hope for this study is . . .

3. The main thing I am afraid of in doing this study is . . .
4. The biggest assumption I am making in my research is . . .
5. The main way that this research draws on my own experience is . . .
6. One thing I'm sure of about what's going on is . . .
7. I would be really surprised if, as a result of the research, I learned . . .

Then, try to identify the issues you've raised that are most likely to be important in your research, think about the implications of these, and organize your reflections more systematically into a memo.

EXERCISE 3.2
Creating a Concept Map for Your Study

How do you develop a concept map? First, you need to have a set of concepts to work with. These can come from existing theory, from your own experience, or from the people you are studying—their own concepts of what's going on (discussed above under Pilot Research). The main thing to keep in mind is that at this point you are trying to represent the theory *you already have* about the phenomena you are studying, not primarily to invent a new theory.

1. *Begin with the thing you want to understand and your tentative understanding of it.* Think about the key words you use in talking about this phenomenon; these probably represent important concepts in your theory. You can pull some of these concepts directly from things you've already written about your research; take your memos and underline the key terms, then use these as your initial categories. Alternatively, you can take one key concept, idea, or term, and brainstorm all of the things that might be related to this, then go back and select those that seem most directly relevant to your study.

2. *Once you've generated some concepts to work with, ask yourself how these are related.* What connections do you see among them? Leigh Star (quoted in Strauss, 1987, p. 179) suggests beginning with one category or concept and drawing "tendrils" to others. What do you think are the important connections between the concepts you're using? The key pieces of a concept map aren't the circles, but the arrows; these represent proposed relationships between the concepts or events. Ask yourself, what do I mean by this particular arrow? What does it stand for? Think of concrete examples of what you're dealing with, rather than working only with abstractions. Don't lock yourself into the first set of categories you select, or the first arrangement you try. Brainstorm different ways of putting the concepts together; move the categories around to see what works best. Ask questions about the diagram, draw possible connections, and ask if they make sense. An alternative strategy is to take something you've already written and try to map the theory that is implicit (or explicit) in this. This is often the best approach for people who don't think visually and prefer to work with prose. Strauss (1987, pp. 182-183) and Miles

and Huberman (1994, p. 22) provide additional advice on how to develop concept maps for your study.

3. *Finally, write a narrative of what this concept map says about the phenomena you are studying.* Try to capture in words the ideas that are embodied in the diagram. Figures 3.3 and 3.4 present concept maps with accompanying narratives; Miles and Huberman (1994, pp. 135-136, 159-161) give additional examples. This is an important part of the exercise; it can point out when something in your map is simply a *placeholder* for the actual concept or relationship that you need and can suggest ways to develop your theory.

NOTES

1. The idea that existing theory and research provide *modules* that you can use in your own research is developed at length by Becker (1986, p. 141ff.).

2. For a detailed account of the ways in which researchers can use theory in formulating their purposes, research questions, and methods, see LeCompte and Preissle (1993, pp. 115-157).

3. Miles and Huberman (1994) tend to refer to variance maps as *causal networks* and process maps as *event-state networks* (pp. 101-171). In my view, this unduly equates causal analysis with variance analysis; process explanations are *also* causal, as discussed in Chapter 2 and illustrated in Figure 3.4.

4

Research Questions: What Do You Want to Understand?

Your research questions—what you specifically want to understand by doing your study—are at the heart of your research design. They are the one component that directly links to all of the other components of the design. More than any other aspect of your design, your research questions will have an influence on, and should be responsive to, every other part of your study.

In most works on research design, however, research questions are presented as the *starting point* or primary determinant of the design. Models of design that place the formulation of research questions at the beginning of the design process, and see these questions as determining the other aspects of the design, don't do justice to the interactive and inductive nature of qualitative research. The research questions in a qualitative study shouldn't be formulated in detail until the purposes and context (and sometimes general aspects of the sampling and data collection) of the design are clarified, and they should remain sensitive and adaptable to the implications of other parts of the design. Often you will need to do a significant part of the research before it is clear what specific research questions you should try to answer.

This doesn't mean that qualitative researchers should, or usually do, begin a study with *no* questions, simply going into the field with an open mind and seeing what is there to be investigated. As discussed in the previous chapter, every researcher begins with a substantial base of experience and theoretical knowledge, and these inevitably generate certain questions about the phenomena studied. These initial questions frame the study in important ways, influence decisions about methods, and are one basis for further focusing and development of more specific questions. My argument is that specific questions are generally the *result* of an interactive design process, rather than being the starting point for that process (see Example 4.1).

EXAMPLE 4.1

The Development of Research Questions

Suman Bhattacharjea's (1994) dissertation dealt with the ways in which the female administrators in an educational district office in Pakistan defined, implemented, and controlled their professional tasks and working environment in a gender-segregated and male-dominated society. She began her fieldwork with a single broad question: "What do staff in this office do every day, and who does what?" Her position as a consultant to a computer implementation project required her to spend much of her time interacting with the women in this office; the fact that she was female, spoke virtually the same language, and (being from India) was familiar with some aspects of their lives led to acceptance and trust. When she submitted her dissertation proposal, a year after she began the research, she had focused her study on two specific questions:

1. What is the nature of the expectations that affect female administrators' actions?
2. What strategies do female administrators adopt to deal with these constraints in the context of a gender-segregated and male-dominated environment?

On the basis of the research she had already done, she was able to formulate three propositions as tentative answers to these questions:

1. Female administrators' actions reflect their desire to *maintain harmony* between their roles as women in a gender-segregated society and their roles as officials within a bureaucracy.
2. The major strategy female administrators use in this regard is to try to create a "family-like" environment at work, interacting with their colleagues in ways that parallel their interactions in a domestic setting and thus blurring the distinction between *public* and *private.*
3. The implications of this strategy for female administrators' actions depend upon the *context* of their interaction, and in particular where this context lies on the public/private continuum. Women use different strategies when interacting with other women (most private or family-like), with male colleagues within the office, and with other men (least private or family-like).

In this chapter, I will discuss the functions of research questions in a research design, consider the *kinds* of questions that a qualitative study can investigate, and give some suggestions on how these questions can be generated.

THE FUNCTIONS OF RESEARCH QUESTIONS

In a research *proposal,* the function of your research questions is to explain specifically what your study will attempt to learn or understand. In your research *design,* the research questions serve two other vital functions: to help you to focus the study (the questions' relationship to your purposes and conceptual context) and to give you guidance on how to conduct it (their relationship to methods and validity) (cf. Miles & Huberman, 1994, pp. 22-25).

A design in which the research questions are too general or too diffuse creates difficulties both in conducting the study—in knowing what site or informants to choose, what data to collect, and how to analyze these data—and in clearly connecting what you do to your purposes and existing knowledge. If your questions remain on the "What's going on here?" level, you have no clear guide in deciding what data to collect, in selecting or generating relevant theory for your study, or in determining if your study is meeting your purposes. Precisely framed research questions, on the other hand, can point you to specific areas of theory that you can use as modules in developing an understanding of what's going on; they allow you to inductively develop and test grounded theory, as well as helping you to make decisions about how you will do the study.

On the other hand, it is possible for your questions to be *too* focused; they may create tunnel vision, leaving out things that are important for the purposes or context of the study. Research questions that are precisely framed too early in the study may lead you to overlook areas of theory or prior experience that are relevant to your understanding of what is going on; they may also cause you to not pay enough attention to a wide range of data early in the study, data that can reveal important and unanticipated phenomena and relationships.

A third problem is that you may be smuggling unexamined assumptions into the research questions themselves, imposing a conceptual framework that doesn't fit the reality you're studying. A research question such as "How do teachers deal with the experience of isolation from their colleagues in their classrooms?" assumes that teachers *do* experience such isolation. Such an assumption needs to be carefully examined and justified, and a question of this form may be better placed as a subquestion to broader questions about the nature of classroom teachers' experience of their work and their relations with colleagues.

Fourth, there is the possibility, an unfortunate but not uncommon one with students beginning to write dissertation proposals, that the research questions bear *no* discernable relationship to the writer's real purposes and actual beliefs about what's going on. Instead, they are sham questions constructed to satisfy what the writer thinks reviewers will want to see in the proposal, and lack any real conceptual or experiential support. In qualitative research, such questions often result from the adoption of quantitative research conventions in ways that are inappropriate for a qualitative study.

For all of these reasons, there is a real danger in not carefully formulating your research questions in connection with the other components of your design. Your research questions need to take account of why you want to do the study (your purposes) and of what is already known about the things you want to study and your tentative theories about these phenomena (your conceptual context). There is no reason to pose research questions for which the answer is already available, or questions that don't clearly connect to what you think is actually going on.

Likewise, your research questions need to be ones that are answerable by the kind of study you could actually conduct. There is no value in posing questions that no feasible study could answer, either because the data that could answer them could not be obtained, or because the conclusions you might draw would be subject to serious validity threats. These issues will be covered in more detail in the next two chapters.

A necessary prerequisite for framing appropriate research questions for your study is to understand clearly what a research question is and the different kinds of research questions that you might pose. I will first discuss the nature of research questions in general and then introduce some specific distinctions among research questions that are particularly important for qualitative studies.

RESEARCH QUESTIONS AND
OTHER KINDS OF QUESTIONS

A common problem in developing research questions is a confusion between research issues—what you want to *understand* by doing the study—and practical issues—what you want to *accomplish*. As discussed in Chapter 2, practical issues are best kept as part of your purposes, rather than being directly incorporated in your research questions. LeCompte and Preissle (1993) state that "distinguishing between the purpose and the research question is the first problem" in coming up with workable research questions (p. 37). This may be a more difficult task than you expect, because it forces you to focus on what you *don't* know about the phenomenon, rather than what you know or assume that you know. It requires you to both identify your ignorance and to critically challenge your assumptions.

A second distinction, one that is critical for interview studies, is between research questions and interview questions. Your research questions identify the things that you want to understand; your interview questions provide the data that you need to understand these things. This distinction is discussed in more detail in Chapter 5.

RESEARCH HYPOTHESES
IN QUALITATIVE DESIGNS

Research questions are not the same as research hypotheses. Research questions state what you want to learn. Hypotheses, in contrast, are a statement of your tentative answers to these questions—what you think is going on. The use of explicit research hypotheses is often seen as incompatible with qualitative research. My view, in contrast, is that there is no inherent problem with formulating qualitative research hypotheses; the difficulty has been partly a matter of terminology and partly a matter of the inappropriate application of quantitative standards to qualitative research hypotheses.

Many qualitative researchers explicitly state their ideas about what is going on as part of the process of theorizing and data analysis. These are often called *propositions* rather than hypotheses (Miles & Huberman, 1994, p. 75), but they serve the same function. The distinctive characteristic of hypotheses in qualitative research is that they are generally formulated *after* the researcher has begun the study; they are grounded in the data and are developed and tested in interaction with it, rather than being prior ideas that are simply tested against data (see Example 4.1).

This runs counter to the view, widespread in quantitative research, that unless a hypothesis is framed in advance of data collection, it can't be legitimately tested by the data. This requirement is essential for the *statistical* test of a hypothesis; if the hypothesis is framed after seeing data, the assumptions of the statistical test are violated. Colloquially, this is referred to as a "fishing expedition"—searching through the data to find what seem to be significant relationships. However, qualitative researchers rarely engage in statistical significance testing, so that this argument is largely irrelevant to qualitative research.

The main drawback of explicitly formulating hypotheses is that, like prior theory, they can act as blinders, preventing you from seeing what's going on. As with prior theory, you need to treat these hypotheses critically, continually asking yourself what alternative ways there are of making sense of your data. Fishing for insights is a perfectly legitimate strategy, as long as these insights are then tested against possible validity threats.

I next want to discuss three specific distinctions among kinds of research questions, ones that are important to consider in developing the questions for your study. These distinctions are between generalizing and particularizing questions, between instrumentalist and realist questions, and between variance and process questions.

GENERALIZING QUESTIONS
AND PARTICULARIZING QUESTIONS

There is a widespread, but often implicit, assumption that research questions should be framed in general terms and then operationalized by means of specific sampling and data collection decisions. For example, there is a strong tendency to state a research question as "How do students deal with racial and ethnic difference in multiracial schools?" and to then operationalize this to a particular school, rather than to state the question at the outset as "How do students at North High School deal with racial and ethnic difference?" I will refer to these two types of questions as generalizing and particularizing questions, respectively.

The assumption that questions should be stated in generalizing terms may derive in large part from experimental psychology, where this is the standard approach. However, it is an assumption that often does not fit research in the social sciences and in fields such as education, where both generalizing and particularizing questions can be appropriate and legitimate. It is especially misleading in applied research, where the focus is usually on understanding and improving some particular program, situation, or practice.

These two types of questions are linked to the difference between a sampling approach and a case study approach to research. In a sample study, the researcher states a generalizing question about a broad population and then selects a particular sample from this population in order to answer the question. In a case study, in contrast, the researcher often selects the case and then states the questions in terms of the particular case selected. A sample study justifies the sampling strategy as a way of attaining what Cook and Campbell (1979) call *statistical conclusion validity*—the representativeness of the specific data collected, and the relationships among these data, for the population sampled. A case study, on the other hand, justifies the selection of a particular case in terms of the purposes of the study and existing theory and research, and a different kind of argument is needed to support the generalizability of its conclusions. (For a discussion of generalizability, see Chapter 6.)

Both approaches are legitimate in qualitative research. Interview-based studies, in particular, often employ a sampling logic, selecting interviewees in order to generalize to some population of interest. In addition, the larger the study, the more feasible and appropriate a sampling approach becomes; large multisite studies (such as those described in Miles & Huberman, 1994) must pay considerable attention to issues of sampling and representativeness. (For more on sampling, see the discussion in Chapter 5.)

However, qualitative studies often employ small samples of uncertain representativeness, and this usually means that the study can provide only suggestive answers to any question framed in general terms, such as "How do kindergarten teachers assess the readiness of children for first grade?" A plausible answer to this generalizing question would normally require some sort of probability sampling from the population of all kindergarten teachers, and a larger sample than most qualitative studies can manage. Furthermore, the phrase "kindergarten teachers" is itself in need of further specification. Does it refer only to American teachers? Only to public school teachers? Only to teachers with several years of experience? These concerns, and analogous ones that could be raised about any research questions framed in generalizing terms, presuppose a sample framework for the study and may push the design in a quantitative direction.

On the other hand, a qualitative study *can* confidently answer such a question posed in particularizing terms, such as "How do the kindergarten teachers *in this school* assess the readiness of children for first grade?" This way of stating the question, although it does not avoid issues of sampling, frames the study much more in case terms. The teachers are treated not as a sample from some much larger population of teachers to whom the study is intended to generalize, but as a *case* of a group of teachers who are studied in a particular context (the specific school and community). The selection of this particular case may involve considerations of representativeness (and certainly any attempt to generalize from the conclusions must take representativeness into account), but the primary concern of the study is not with generalization but with developing an adequate description, interpretation, and theory of this case.

INSTRUMENTALIST QUESTIONS
AND REALIST QUESTIONS

Social science was long dominated by the positivist view that all theoretical terms should be precisely defined in terms of research operations and objective data. Although this view has been abandoned by almost all philosophers of science, it still influences the way many researchers think about research questions. Advisers and reviewers often recommend framing research questions in terms of what the respondents say or report, or in terms of what can be directly observed, rather than in terms of inferred behavior, psychological states, or causal influences.

For example, Gail Lenehan, for her dissertation, proposed to interview nurses who specialize in treating sexual assault victims about their cognitive, behavioral, and emotional reactions to this work. Although there is considerable anecdotal evidence that these nurses often experience reactions similar to those of their victims, no one had systematically studied this phenomenon. Her research questions included the following:

1. What, if any, are the effects on nurses of working with rape victims?
2. Are there cognitive, psychological, and behavioral responses to having experiences of rape "shared" with them, as well as witnessing victims' suffering after the assault?

Her proposal was not accepted, and the reviewers, in explaining their decision, argued (among other concerns) that

> the study relies solely on self-report data, but your questions do not reflect this limitation. Each question needs to be reframed in terms that reflect this limitation. Some examples might be: "How do nurses perceive and report . . . the effects of working with rape victims?" or "What specific cognitive, psychological (emotional?), and behavioral responses do nurses report?"

This disagreement illustrates the difference between instrumentalist and realist approaches (Norris, 1983) to research questions. Instrumentalists formulate their questions in terms of observable or measurable data. They worry about the potential validity threats (such as self-report bias) that inference to unobservable phenomena entails, and prefer to stick with what they can directly verify. Realists, in contrast, do not assume that research questions and conclusions about feelings, beliefs, intentions, prior behavior, effects, and so on need to be reduced to, or reframed as, questions and conclusions about the actual data that one uses. Instead, they treat their data as fallible *evidence* about these phenomena, to be used critically to develop and test ideas about the existence and nature of the phenomena (Campbell, 1988; Cook & Campbell, 1979; Maxwell, 1992).

This is not a matter of philosophical hair-splitting; it has important implications for how you will do the research, and each of the two approaches has its risks. The main risk of instrumentalist questions is that you will lose sight of what you're really interested in and define your study in ways that obscure the actual phenomena you want to investigate, ending up with a rigorous but uninteresting conclusion. As in the joke about the man who was looking for his keys under the streetlight (rather than where he dropped them) because the light was better there, you may never find what you started out to look for. An instrumentalist approach to your research questions may also make it more difficult for your study to directly address important purposes of your study (such as developing programs to deal with the actual effects on nurses of talking to rape victims), and it can inhibit your theorizing about phenomena that are not directly observable.

The main risk with realist questions, on the other hand, is that your increased reliance on inference may lead you to draw unwarranted conclusions or to allow your assumptions or desires to influence your results. My own preference is to use realist questions and to address as systematically and rigorously as possible the validity threats that this approach involves. I have several reasons for this. First, the seriousness of these validity threats (such as self-report bias) depends on the topic, goals, and methods of the research and thus needs to be assessed in the context of a particular study; these threats are often not as serious as instrumentalists imply. Second, there are usually effective ways to address these threats in a qualitative design; these will be discussed in Chapter 6. The risk of trivializing your study by restricting your questions to what can be directly observed is usually more serious than the risk of drawing invalid conclusions. What statistician John Tukey (1962) said about precision is also true of certainty: "Far better an approximate answer to the right question, which is often vague, than an exact answer to the wrong question, which can always be made precise" (p. 13; cited in Light & Pillemer, 1984, p. 105).

My advice to students in Lenehan's position is to argue for the legitimacy of framing your questions in realist terms (which she successfully did). Even if you are required to restrict your *proposal* to instrumentalist questions, you should make sure that your actual *design* incorporates any realist concerns that you want your study to address.

One issue that is not entirely a matter of realism versus instrumentalism is whether research questions in interview studies should be framed in terms of the respondents' perceptions or beliefs, rather than the actual state of affairs. This is an issue for Lenehan's study, described above; one recommendation of the reviewers was to focus the questions on how nurses *perceive* the effects of working with rape victims, rather than on the actual effects. Although both of these are in principle realist questions, because neither is something that can be directly derived from interview data, there is a definite instrumentalist bias in the reviewers' advice, because inferences to the actual situation or behavior being reported are in most circumstances more indirect and problematic than are inferences to the perspective of the respondent.

This decision should be based not simply on the seriousness of the validity threats but also on what you actually want to understand. In many qualitative studies, the real interest is in how participants make sense of what has happened, and how this perspective informs their actions, rather than determining precisely what they did. (This is essentially the difference between interpretation and description, discussed in Chapter 2.)

VARIANCE QUESTIONS
AND PROCESS QUESTIONS

Finally, I want to return to the distinction between variance theory and process theory that I raised in Chapter 2 and relate this to the framing of research questions. Variance questions focus on difference and correlation; they often begin with "Does," "How much," "To what extent," and "Is there." Process questions, in contrast, focus on *how* things happen, rather than whether there is a particular relationship or how much it is explained by other variables. The fundamental distinction here is between questions that focus on differences and those that focus on processes.

For example, asking "Do more adopted women than adopted men place importance on finding their birth mothers, and if so, why?" is a variance question, because it implies a search for a difference and for the particular variables that explain the difference. An example of a process question would be "Why do adopted women (or men, or both) place importance on finding their birth mothers?" The focus in the latter question is not in explaining a difference (a dependent variable) in terms of some independent variables, but on understanding how adopted individuals think about and act on the knowledge that they are adopted. The two questions involve different uses of the term *why;* both are explanations, but they are different kinds of explanations.

In a qualitative study, it can be dangerous for you to frame your research questions in a way that focuses on differences and their explanation. This may lead you to begin thinking in variance terms, to try to identify the variables that will account for observed or hypothesized differences, and to overlook the real strength of a qualitative approach, which is in understanding the process by which phenomena take place. Variance questions are often best answered by quantitative approaches, which are powerful ways of determining *whether* a particular result was causally related to one or another variable, and to *what extent* these are related. However, qualitative research is often better at showing *how* this occurred. (See the discussion of causality in Chapter 2.) Variance questions are legitimate in qualitative research, but they are often best grounded in the answers to prior process questions.

Qualitative researchers thus tend to focus on two kinds of questions that are much better suited to process theory than to variance theory: questions about the *meaning* of events and activities to the people involved in these, and questions about the influence of the physical and social *context* on these events and activities. (See the discussion of meaning and context as purposes of qualitative research in Chapter 2.) Because both of these types of questions involve situation-specific phenomena, they do not lend themselves to the kinds of comparison and control that variance theory requires. Instead, they generally involve an open-ended, inductive approach, in order to discover what these meanings and influences are and how they are involved in these events and activities—an inherently processual orientation.

TYPES OF UNDERSTANDING
IN QUALITATIVE RESEARCH

An additional consideration in framing research questions is the kinds of understanding that your study can generate. I have elsewhere defined five categories of understanding in qualitative research, which I have called description, interpretation, theory, generalization, and evaluation (Maxwell, 1992), and in Chapter 2, I gave a brief explanation of description, interpretation, and theory. I raise these categories here because each category has its own type of research question. Descriptive questions ask about what actually happened in terms of observable (or potentially observable) behavior or events. Interpretive questions, in contrast, ask about the meaning of these things for the people involved: their thoughts, feelings, and intentions. Theoretical questions ask about *why* these things happened, how they can be explained. These three categories include most of the types of questions that qualitative researchers develop. Research questions that specifically address the generality or wider prevalence of the phenomena studied, or how such phenomena should be evaluated, are normally not appropriate for a qualitative study, the former because qualitative studies rarely involve the sampling procedures or sample size necessary to directly address generalizability, and the latter because explicitly evaluative questions create a serious risk that you will impose your own values and ignore those of the people you study. This does not mean that you can never generalize or evaluate on the basis of a qualitative study (see Chapter 6 for a discussion of generalizability, and Patton, 1990, on evaluation), only that such concerns are usually best *not* incorporated directly into your research questions. Evaluation in particular should usually be kept as part of your purposes and addressed in discussing the implications of your study.

DEVELOPING RESEARCH QUESTIONS

Light et al. (1990) point out that formulating research questions is not a simple or straightforward task:

> Do not expect to expect to sit down for an hour and produce an elaborate list of specific questions. Although you must take the time to do just that—sit down and write—your initial list will not be your final list. Expect to iterate. A good set of research questions will evolve, over time, after you have considered and reconsidered your broad research theme. (p. 19)

And they warn, "Be wary of the desire to push forward before going through this process" (p. 19).

Exercise 4.1 offers a guide for you to work through in developing your research questions. This exercise will not only generate research questions; it will also help you connect these questions to the other four components of your research design, in order to make these questions as relevant and practicable as possible. These connections are two-way streets; try to see not only what questions, or changes in questions, the other four components suggest, but also what changes in these other components your questions imply.

EXERCISE 4.1
Developing Your Research Questions

1. *Begin by setting aside whatever research questions you already have and starting with your concept map* (Chapter 3). What are the places in this map that you don't understand adequately, or where you need to test your ideas? Where are the holes in, or conflicts between, your experiential knowledge and existing theories, and what questions do these imply? Try to write down all of the potential questions that you can draw from the map.

2. *Next, take your original research questions and compare them to the map and the questions you generated from it.* What would answering these questions tell you that you don't already know? What changes or additions to your questions does your map suggest? Conversely, are there places where your original questions imply things that should be on your map, but aren't? What changes do you need to make to your map?

3. *Now go through the same process with the memo you wrote on your purposes* (Chapter 2). What would you need to know in order to accomplish these purposes? What questions does this imply? Conversely, how do your original questions connect to your reasons for conducting the study? How will answering these *specific* questions help you to achieve your purposes? Which questions are most interesting to you personally, practically, or intellectually?

4. *Now focus.* What questions are most central to your study? How do these questions form a coherent set that will guide your study? You can't study everything interesting about your topic; start making choices. Three or four main questions is usually a reasonable maximum for a qualitative study, although you can have additional subquestions for each of the main questions.

In addition, you need to carefully consider whether your planned study can actually answer the questions you pose. At this point in your planning, this may primarily involve thought experiments about the way you will conduct the study, the kinds of data you will collect, and the analyses you will perform on these data. This part of the exercise is one you can usefully repeat when you have developed your methods and validity concerns in more detail; Exercise 5.2, in the next chapter, also addresses these issues.

5. *Connect your questions to the methods you might use.* Could your questions be answered by these methods and the data that they would provide? What methods would you need to use to collect data that would answer these questions? Conversely, what questions can a qualitative study of the kind you are planning productively address?

6. *Assess the potential answers to your questions in terms of validity.* What are the plausible validity threats and alternative explanations that you would have to rule out? How might you be wrong, and what implications does this have for the way you frame your questions?

Finally, record your responses and the thoughts they provoked in a memo.

An extremely valuable additional step is to share your questions and your reflections on these with one or more fellow students or colleagues. Ask them if they understand the questions and why these would be worth answering, what other questions or changes in the questions they would suggest, and what problems they see in trying to answer them. If possible, tape record the discussion; afterward, listen to the tape and take notes.

I recommend that, unless you find visual representations particularly unhelpful, you try *diagramming* the relationships among your design components, as a concept map of the current design of your study. This can help you to see the design as a whole, and particular connections within it, more clearly than by using a narrative presentation alone. Figure 4.1. is a concept map of the design of Maria Broderick's research, which was described in Example 1.1.

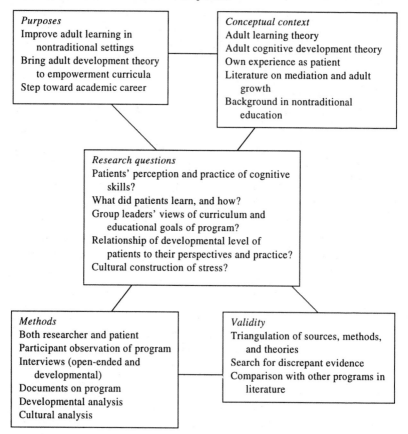

Figure 4.1. Final Design of Maria Broderick's Research

5

Methods:
What Will You Actually Do?

In this chapter, I discuss some of the key issues involved in deciding what you will do in conducting your research. The focus is on how to *design* a qualitative study, not on the skills you need to actually do qualitative research. I am assuming that you already know (or are learning) how to use the methods discussed here in carrying out your study. These methods are not limited to the techniques of qualitative data collection (primarily participant observation and interviewing) but also include establishing a research relationship with those you study and analyzing the data that you collect.

I want to emphasize that there is no "cookbook" for doing qualitative research. The appropriate answer to almost any question about the use of qualitative methods is "it depends." The value and practicability of your research methods cannot be guaranteed by adhering to methodological rules; they depend on the specific setting and phenomena you are studying and the actual consequences of your strategy for studying these. What I want to discuss here are some of the things that your methodological decisions depend *on,* issues that you will need to think about in designing your research methods.

PRESTRUCTURING A
QUALITATIVE STUDY

One of the most important issues in designing a qualitative study is how much you should attempt to prestructure your methods. Many qualitative researchers believe that, because qualitative research is necessarily inductive and grounded, any significant prestructuring of the methods leads to a lack of flexibility to respond to emergent insights and creates methodological blinders in making sense of the data. This decision is often justified on philosophical or political grounds, as well; structured approaches are identified with quantitative research, positivism, or power inequalities between the researcher and the researched. The choice between structured and unstructured methods is rarely discussed in a way that clarifies the relative advantages and disadvantages of each. (Significant exceptions are Miles & Huberman, 1994; Robson, 1993; Sayer, 1992.)

Structured approaches can help to ensure the comparability of data across sources and researchers and are thus particularly useful in answering variance questions, questions that deal with *differences* between things and their explanation. Unstructured approaches, in contrast, allow the researcher to focus on the *particular* phenomena studied; they trade generalizability and comparability for internal validity and contextual understanding and are particularly useful in understanding the processes that led to specific outcomes, what Huberman and Miles (1985/1988) call *local causality.* Sayer (1992, p. 241ff.) refers to these two approaches as *extensive* and *intensive* research designs, respectively.

However, Miles and Huberman (1994) warn that

> highly inductive, loosely designed studies make good sense when experienced researchers have plenty of time and are exploring exotic cultures, understudied phenomena, or very complex social phenomena. But if you're new to qualitative studies and are looking at a better understood phenomenon within a familiar culture or subculture, a loose, inductive design is a waste of time. Months of fieldwork and voluminous case studies may yield only a few banalities. (p. 17)

They also point out that prestructuring reduces the amount of data that you have to deal with, functioning as a form of preanalysis that simplifies the analytic work required.

In general, I agree with Miles and Huberman's assessment, although I think their involvement with multiple-site research has led them to advocate more prestructuring than is appropriate for most single-site studies. However, like nearly everyone else, they treat prestructuring as a single dimension and view it in terms of metaphors such as hard versus soft and tight versus loose. Such metaphors, in addition to their one-dimensional implications, have powerful value connotations (although these are different for different people) that can interfere with your assessment of the tradeoffs involved in particular design decisions and the best ways to combine different forms of prestructuring within a single design (cf. Lakoff & Johnson, 1980). These metaphors can lead you to overlook or ignore the numerous ways in which studies can vary, not just in the *amount* of prestructuring, but in *how* prestructuring is used.[1]

For example, Festinger, Riecker, and Schachter (1956), in a well-known social psychology study of an end-of-the-world cult, employed an extremely open approach to data collection, relying primarily on descriptive fieldnotes from covert participant observation in the cult. However, they used these data to conduct a confirmatory test of explicit hypotheses based on a prior theory, rather than to inductively develop new questions or theory. In contrast, the approach often known as ethnoscience or cognitive anthropology (Spradley, 1979; Werner & Schoepfle, 1987) employs highly structured data collection techniques but interprets these data in a largely inductive manner, with very few preestablished categories. Thus, the decision you face is not primarily whether or to what extent you prestructure your study, but in what ways you do this, and why.

Finally, it is worth keeping in mind that you can lay out a tentative plan for some aspects of your study in considerable detail but leave open the possibility of substantially revising this if necessary. (See the evolution of Maria Broderick's research design, presented in Chapter 1.) The degree to which you structure your anticipated research methods is a separate decision from how much flexibility you leave yourself to revise the plan during your study. Emergent insights may require new sampling plans, different kinds of data, and different analytic strategies.

As stated earlier, all research has an implicit, if not explicit, research design. Avoiding decisions about your design may mean only that you aren't examining the design that is implicit in your thinking and are failing to recognize the significant implications that these implicit decisions will have. Deliberate attention to these implications can help you to construct a design that will enable you to answer your questions and advance your purposes, and possibly save you a lot of trouble.

I see qualitative methods—what you will actually do in conducting a qualitative study—as having four main components. These are:

1. The research relationship that you establish with those you study
2. Sampling: what times, settings, or individuals you select to observe or interview and what other sources of information you decide to use
3. Data collection: how you gather the information you will use
4. Data analysis: what you do with this information in order to make sense of it

This is a considerably broader definition of methods than is usual in discussions of research design. My justification for this definition is that all of these components are important aspects of how you conduct your study, and affect the value and validity of your conclusions. It is therefore useful to think about these as *design* decisions—key issues that you should consider in planning your study, and that you should rethink as you are engaged in it. In the rest of this chapter, I will discuss what I see as the most important considerations that should affect your decisions about each of these components.

NEGOTIATING A
RESEARCH RELATIONSHIP

The research relationship that you create with those you study is often conceptualized as *gaining entry* to the setting, or *establishing rapport* with your research participants. I think that these are misleading ways of thinking about this aspect of your research, and I will discuss why I think so before going on to the considerations involved in negotiating a research relationship.

The terms *negotiating entry* (Marshall & Rossman, 1994) or *gaining access* (Bogdan & Biklen, 1992; Glesne & Peshkin, 1992) suggest that this is a single event that, once achieved, requires no further thought; these terms downplay the continual negotiation and renegotiation of your relationship with those you study.[2] Clearly the process is much more complex than this and rarely involves any approximation to total access. Nor is such access usually necessary for a successful study; what you want is a relationship that enables you to ethically learn the things you need to learn in order to validly answer your research questions.

Conceptualizing the relationship in terms of *rapport* (e.g., Seidman, 1991, pp. 73-75) is also problematic, because it treats the relationship as a single continuous variable, rather than emphasizing the nature of the relationship. Seidman's point—that it is possible to have too much rapport, as well as too little—is an important one, but I would add that it is the *kind* of rapport, as well as the amount, that is critical. An informant can be very engaged intellectually in an interview but not be revealing anything deeply personal, and for some studies, this kind of relationship may be ideal. Conversely, people may be very open about personal matters to strangers whom they never expect to see again but may not be willing to engage in any critical reflection on this material.

Your relationship with those you study is a complex and changing entity. In qualitative studies, the researcher is the instrument of the research, and the research relationship is the means by which the research gets done. This relationship has an effect not only on the participants in the study, but on the researcher and on other parts of the research design. Hammersley and Atkinson (1983) use the term *reflexivity* to label the recognition that the researcher is inextricably part of the phenomena studied, and argue that

> once we abandon the idea that the social character of research can be standardized out or avoided by becoming a "fly on the wall" or a "full participant," the role of the researcher as active participant in the research process becomes clear. (p. 18)

In particular, the research relationship you establish can facilitate or hinder other components of the research design such as sampling and data collection methods. For example, in my dissertation research in an Inuit community, I made arrangements to live with different families on a monthly basis. This gave me access to detailed information about a wider range of families than is often available to anthropologists, who typically establish close ties with a small number of individuals or families. However, the ways in which this arrangement was negotiated made it difficult for me to develop working relationships with those families with whom I did not live (Maxwell, 1986). Rabinow (1977) provides an insightful account of the way in which his changing relationships with his Moroccan informants affected his research plans, and Bosk (1979) explains how his relationships with the surgeons he studied both facilitated and constrained his research. Briggs (1986) describes how his relationship with his Mexicano hosts in a New Mexico village both precluded the kinds of interviews he had planned to conduct and taught him a great deal about the culturally appropriate ways to gain information in this village. Many other accounts by qualitative researchers of their research provide similar insights; rather than attempting to sum these up in a few, only partially generalizable guidelines, I urge you to read widely in the literature on this topic, so that your decisions can be informed by a range of other researchers' experiences.

Thus, it is important to think about the kind of relationship you want to have with the people whom you study, as well as what you need to do to establish this relationship. I want to reiterate that these are *design decisions*, not simply something that happens in the study. The "what you need to do" question gets deeper into issues of qualitative methods than this book can cover, but you will need to reflect on the particular decisions you make about your relationships with those you study and the effects these can have on your research.

In addition to these considerations, there are philosophical, ethical, and political issues that should inform the kind of relationship that you want to

---

EXAMPLE 5.1

Negotiating Relationships in
a Practitioner Research Study

Bobby Starnes, a doctoral student with extensive experience as a teacher and administrator and with a longtime political commitment to collaborative decision making, came to the Harvard Graduate School of Education to see how her knowledge of teaching and learning with children could inform her work with adults. While she was seeking a dissertation study that would allow her to apply and test her ideas, she was hired as director of a day care center serving a low-income population, a center that had a history of ineffective, top-down management. Her dissertation research was a study of what happened when she attempted to implement a system of shared decision making in this setting—how the system evolved and how it affected staff morale, competence, and performance.

Bobby's study required her to have a very different relationship with her study participants than that found in most research; she was both their boss and a researcher trying to understand their perspective on the organizational changes she instituted. In addition, her political views led her to design a study in which she was engaged in real-world action to improve people's lives, not ivory-tower research. This combination posed substantial risks of bias and distortion of the data, as well as unique opportunities for understanding the process of organizational change. It was thus absolutely essential for her study that her participants be open about their perceptions and feelings and that they trust her not to use the data she collected in ways that would be harmful to them.

Bobby was able to accomplish this by establishing an organizational climate in which staff members were not afraid to voice their opinions and disagree with her and in which they were convinced that she would not violate confidences or take action against them as a result of what she learned. (Obviously, this was not an easy task and required all of her skill and experience to carry out; for a detailed description of how she did this, see Starnes, 1990.) Without this relationship, the conclusions of her study would not have been trustworthy. However, she did not assume that the relationship that she had with her staff would automatically eliminate problems of distortion and concealment. She gathered some data by anonymous questionnaires and had another researcher conduct half of the final interviews.

---

establish. In recent years, the dominance of the traditional research relationship has been challenged by alternative modes of research that involve quite different sorts of relationships between the researcher and the researched—in some cases, breaking down this distinction entirely. These alternative modes include qualitative evaluation (Greene, 1994; Patton, 1990; Pitman & Maxwell, 1992), participatory action research (Whyte, 1991), collaborative research (Oja & Smulyan, 1989; Reason, 1988, 1994; Schensul & Schensul, 1992), constructivist research (Guba & Lincoln, 1989), critical ethnography (Anderson, 1989; Carspecken & Apple, 1992; Kincheloe & McLaren, 1994; Quantz, 1992), feminist research (Nielsen, 1990; Oleson, 1994; Reinharz, 1992; Roman, 1992), and practitioner research (Anderson et al. 1994). Each of these modes of research has its own purposes and theoretical and ethical commitments, and these have different implications for the kind of relationship that the researcher creates with participants in the research (see Example 5.1).

Because the impact of these issues is particular to each individual study, the best strategy for dealing with them is to think about them in the context of your own research. Exercise 5.1 should help you to do this.

DECISIONS ABOUT SAMPLING:
WHERE, WHEN, WHO, AND WHAT

Whenever you have a choice about when and where to observe, who to talk to, or what information sources to focus on, you are faced with a sampling decision. Even a single case study involves a choice of this case rather than others, as well as requiring sampling decisions *within* the case itself. Miles and Huberman (1984) ask, "Knowing, then, that one cannot study everyone everywhere doing everything, even within a single case, how does one limit the parameters of a study?" (p. 36). They go on to argue that

> just *thinking* in sampling-frame terms is healthy methodological medicine. If you are talking with one kind of informant, you need to consider *why* this kind of informant is important, and, from there, which *other* people should be interviewed. This is a good, bias-controlling exercise.
>
> Remember that you are not only sampling *people*, but also *settings, events, and processes*. It is important to line up these parameters with the research questions as well, and to consider whether your choices are doing a representative, time-efficient job of answering them. The settings, events, or processes that come rapidly to mind at the start of the study may not be the most pertinent or data-rich ones. A systematic review can sharpen early and later choices. (p. 41)

Miles and Huberman (1994, pp. 27-34) and LeCompte and Preissle (1993, pp. 56-85) provide valuable discussions of the whole issue of sampling decisions, and I will not repeat all of their points here. Instead, I want to talk about the *kinds* of sampling that you can do, and some of the considerations that are relevant to these decisions.

Discussions of quantitative research design generally consider only two types of sampling: probability sampling and convenience sampling (e.g., Light et al., 1990, p. 56). In probability sampling, each member of the population has a known, non-zero probability of being chosen, allowing statistical generalization from the sample to the population of interest. Light et al. (1990) argue that "probability samples are a paragon of high-quality research" (p. 56), a view that is widespread. As a result, any sampling strategy other than simple or stratified random sampling has been seen as *convenience sampling* and is strongly discouraged.

For qualitative research, this view ignores the fact that most sampling in qualitative research is neither probability sampling nor convenience sampling but falls into a third category: *purposeful sampling* (Patton, 1990, p. 169ff.) or what LeCompte and Preissle (1993, p. 69) call *criterion-based selection*. This is a strategy in which particular settings, persons, or events are selected deliberately in order to provide important information that can't be gotten as well from other choices. For example, Weiss (1994) argues that many qualitative interview studies do not use samples at all, but *panels*: "people who are uniquely able to be informative because they are expert in an area or were privileged witnesses to an event" (p. 17); this is one form of purposeful sampling. Selecting those times, settings, and individuals that can provide you with the information that you need in order to answer your research questions is the most important consideration in qualitative sampling decisions.

Patton (1990) describes 15 different types of sampling that can be employed in qualitative research, almost all of which are forms of purposeful sampling; he mentions convenience sampling only to warn against its use, claiming that

> while convenience and cost are real considerations, they should be the last factors to be taken into account after strategically deliberating on how to get the most information of the greatest utility from the limited number of cases to be sampled. . . . *Convenience sampling is neither purposeful nor strategic.* (p. 181)

However, Weiss (1994, pp. 24-29) argues that there are situations in which convenience sampling is the only feasible way to proceed—for example, in attempting to learn about a group that is difficult to gain access to, or a category of people who are relatively rare in the population and for whom no data on membership exist, such as "house husbands." He lists several strategies for maximizing the value of such convenience samples.[3]

In qualitative studies with large sample sizes (e.g., Huberman, 1989/ 1993) in which generalizability is an important goal, random sampling is a valid and often appropriate procedure. However, simple random sampling is a poor way to draw a small sample, due to the high likelihood of chance variation. Most of the advantages of randomization depend on a reasonably large sample size to make such variations unlikely. Light et al. (1990), in discussing site selection, state that "with only a limited number of sites, consider *purposeful selection,* rather than relying on the idiosyncrasies of chance" (p. 53); the same logic applies to selecting informants and observations.

There are occasional circumstances in which randomization can be useful in a small-scale qualitative study. Bobby Starnes, in her study of shared decision making in a day care center (Example 5.1), used stratified random sampling of center staff when she had more volunteers than she could interview. In this case, a key purpose of randomization was to avoid the perception of favoritism in selecting interviewees. However, in one case, she altered the random selection in order to include a point of view that she believed would not otherwise have been represented (Starnes, 1990, p. 33).

There are at least four possible goals for purposeful sampling. The first is achieving representativeness or typicality of the settings, individuals, or activities selected. Because, as noted above, random sampling is likely to achieve this only with a large sample size, it usually makes more sense in a small-scale study to deliberately select cases, individuals, or situations that are known to be typical. A small sample that has been systematically selected for typicality and relative homogeneity provides far more confidence that the conclusions adequately represent the average members of the population than does a sample of the same size that incorporates substantial random or accidental variation.

The second goal that purposeful sampling can achieve is the opposite of the first—to adequately capture the heterogeneity in the population. The purpose here is to ensure that the conclusions adequately represent the entire *range* of variation, rather than only the typical members or some subset of this range; Guba and Lincoln (1989; cf. Miles & Huberman, 1994) refer to this as *maximum variation* sampling. This is best done by defining the dimensions of variation in the population that are most relevant to your study and systematically selecting individuals, times, or settings that represent the most important possible variations on these dimensions. This process resembles that used for stratified random sampling; the main difference is that the final selection is purposeful rather than random. The trade-off between this approach and selecting a more homogeneous sample is that you have less data about any *particular* kind of case, setting, or individual within the study and will not be able to say as much in depth about typical or modal instances.

The third possible goal is to select your sample to deliberately examine cases that are critical for the theories that you began the study with, or that you have subsequently developed. Extreme cases often provide a crucial test of these theories and can illuminate what is going on in a way that representative cases cannot. For example, Wievorka (1992) describes a study in which the researcher, in order to test the view that the working class was not being assimilated into middle-class society, selected a case that would be highly unfavorable to this position: workers who were extremely affluent. The finding that these workers still retained a clear working-class identity provided far more convincing support for his conclusions than a study of "typical" workers would.[4]

A fourth goal in purposeful sampling can be to establish particular comparisons to illuminate the reasons for differences between settings or individuals. Although such comparisons are less common in qualitative research than in other approaches, the use of *controlled comparison* has a long and respected history in anthropology (Eggan, 1954; Maxwell, 1978; Maxwell, Sandlow, & Bashook, 1986/1987) and is common in multicase qualitative studies.

In many situations, sampling decisions require considerable knowledge of the setting of the study. In Jane Margolis's (1990) study of classroom discourse norms in a college department, she could only interview a small percentage of the students and needed to develop some criteria for selecting a sample. Her committee (of which I was a member) recommended that she interview sophomores and seniors, believing that this would provide the optimal diversity of views. When she consulted with members of the department, however, they told her that sophomores were too new to the department to fully understand the norms of discourse, whereas seniors were too deeply involved in their theses and in planning for graduation to be good informants. Juniors turned out to be the only appropriate choice.

Sampling decisions should also take into account your research relationship with study participants, the feasibility of data collection, validity concerns, and ethics. For example, in Martha Regan-Smith's study of how medical school teachers help students learn basic science (Appendix A), her choice of four award-winning teachers was only based in part on the fact that these teachers were the most likely to exhibit the phenomena she was interested in; another reason was that (as a fellow award winner), she had a close and collegial relationship with them that would facilitate the study. In addition, as exemplary teachers, they would be more likely to be candid about their teaching, and the research would be less likely to create ethical problems arising from her discovery of potentially damaging information about them.

One particular sampling problem in qualitative studies has been called *key informant bias.* Qualitative researchers sometimes rely on a small number of informants for a major part of their data, and even when these informants are purposefully selected and the data themselves seem valid, there is no guarantee that these informants' views are typical. In addition, Poggie (1972) presents evidence that key informants themselves assume greater uniformity than actually exists. There is increasing agreement that cultural groups incorporate substantial diversity and that homogeneity cannot be assumed (Hannerz, 1992; Maxwell, 1995, 1996a). Pelto and Pelto (1975) conclude that "there is often a systematic bias in fieldwork data gathered by means of key informant interviewing" (p. 7). Thus, you need to do systematic sampling in order to be able to claim that key informants' statements are representative of the group as a whole (Heider, 1972; Sankoff, 1971).

DECISIONS ABOUT DATA COLLECTION

Most qualitative methods texts devote considerable space to the strengths and limitations of different qualitative data collection methods (see particularly Bogdan & Biklen, 1992; Patton, 1990), and I don't want to repeat these discussions here. Instead, I want to address two key conceptual issues in selecting and using different data collection methods: the relationship between research questions and data collection methods and the triangulation of different methods. (The relative advantages of structured and unstructured methods, discussed above, are also an important consideration in planning data collection methods.)

The Relationship Between Research Questions and Data Collection Methods

The point that I want to emphasize here is that there is no necessary similarity or deductive relationship between your research questions and the methods you use to collect your data (including your interview questions); the two are distinct and separate parts of your design. This can be a source of confusion, because researchers often talk about "operationalizing" their research questions, or of "translating" the research questions into interview questions. Such language is a vestige of logical positivist views of the relationship between theory and data, views that have been almost completely abandoned by philosophers (Phillips, 1987). The practical consequence of this philosophical shift is that there is no way to logically or mechanically convert research questions into methods; your methods are the means to answering your research questions, not a logical transformation of the latter. Their selection depends not only on your research questions but on the actual research situation and what will work most effectively in that situation to give you the data you need.

A striking example of this is provided by Kirk and Miller (1986, pp. 25-26), who conducted research in Peru on the use of coca leaves. Their open-ended questions about coca use, drawn fairly directly from their research questions, elicited a uniform, limited set of beliefs and practices that simply confirmed the things they had already read about coca. Frustrated and getting desperate, they began asking nonsensical questions, such as "When do you give coca to animals?" or "How did you discover that you didn't like coca?" Taken off guard, their informants began to open up and talk about their personal experience with coca, which was far more extensive that the previous data would have indicated.

This is an extreme case, but it holds in principle for any study. Your research questions formulate what you want to understand; your *interview* questions are what you ask people in order to gain that understanding. The latter are judged not by whether they resemble the research questions, but by whether they provide the data that will contribute to answering these questions. The development of good interview questions requires creativity and insight, rather than a mechanical translation of the research questions into an interview guide; it depends fundamentally on how the interview questions actually work in practice.

This doesn't mean that you should conceal your research questions from your informants or deceive them about what you really want to understand. Carol Gilligan (personal communication) emphasizes the value of asking your informants "real questions," ones to which you are genuinely interested in the answer, rather than contrived questions designed to elicit particular sorts of data. However, these real questions will generally be far more context-specific and diverse than the broad, general research questions that define what you seek to understand in conducting the study. (The main exception to this generalization is when you are collaborating closely with an informant, when it may well be productive to have a sustained dialogue about your research questions.)

There are two important implications of this lack of similarity between research questions and interview questions. First, you need to anticipate, as best you can, how particular interview questions will actually work in practice—how people will understand them and how they are likely to respond. Try to put yourself in your informants' place and imagine how you would react to these questions. (This is another use of thought experiments.) Second, if at all possible, you should pilot-test your interview guide with people as much like your planned informants as possible, to determine if the questions work as intended and what revisions you will need to make.

This lack of isomorphism between questions and methods also holds for observation and other methods. As with interviews, you need to anticipate what information you will actually be able to collect in the setting studied, using particular observational or other methods, and if possible you should pretest these methods to determine if they will actually provide this information. Your data collection strategies will probably go through a lengthy period of focusing and revision, even in a carefully designed study, to make sure that they are providing the data that you need to answer your research questions and to address any plausible validity threats to these answers.

Triangulation of Data Collection Methods

Dexter (1970) argues that

> no one should plan or finance an entire study in advance with the expectation of relying chiefly upon interviews for data unless the interviewers have enough relevant background to be sure that they can make sense out of interview conversations or unless there is a reasonable hope of being able to hang around or in some way observe so as to learn what it is meaningful and significant to ask. (p. 17)

This example illustrates the general principle known as triangulation: collecting information from a diverse range of individuals and settings, using a variety of methods (Denzin, 1970). This reduces the risk that your conclusions will reflect only the systematic biases or limitations of a specific method, and it allows you to gain a better assessment of the validity and generality of the explanations that you develop. (I discuss the use of triangulation to deal with validity threats in Chapter 6.)

Bobby Starnes's study (Example 5.1) provides a good illustration of the use of triangulation. She used four sources of data (the direct care staff, her administrative team, her own notes and journals, and center records) and several different methods of collecting these data. For example, the data from the staff were collected through journals, formal and informal interviews, participation in center activities, and anonymous questionnaires. These multiple sources and methods give her conclusions far more credibility than if she had been limited to one source or method.

One belief that inhibits triangulation is the widespread assumption that observation is mainly useful for obtaining descriptions of behavior and events, whereas interviewing is mainly useful for obtaining the perspectives of actors. It is true that the *immediate* result of observation is description, but this is equally true of interviewing: the latter gives you a description of what informants *said,* not a direct understanding of their perspective. Generating an interpretation of someone's perspective is inherently a matter of inference from descriptions of his or her behavior (including verbal behavior), whether the data are derived from observations, interviews, or some other source such as written documents (Maxwell, 1992).

Observation often enables you to draw inferences about someone's meaning and perspective that you couldn't obtain by relying exclusively on interview data. This is particularly true for getting at tacit understandings and *theory-in-use,* as well as aspects of the participants' perspective that they are reluctant to state directly in interviews. For example, watching how a teacher responds to boys' and girls' questions in a science class may provide a much better understanding of the teacher's actual views about gender and science than what the teacher says in an interview.

Conversely, interviewing can be a valuable way (the only way, for events that took place in the past or ones to which you cannot gain observational access) of gaining a description of actions and events. These can provide additional information that was missed in observation and can be used to check the accuracy of the observations. However, in order for interviewing to be useful for this purpose, you need to ask about specific events and actions, rather than posing questions that elicit only generalizations or abstract opinions (Weiss, 1994, pp. 72-76). In both of these cases, triangulation of observations and interviews can provide a more complete and accurate account than either could alone.

DECISIONS ABOUT DATA ANALYSIS

Analysis is often conceptually separated from design, especially by writers who see design as what happens *before* the data are actually collected. Here, I treat analysis as a part of design, and as something that must itself be designed. Any qualitative study requires decisions about how the analysis will be done, and these decisions should influence, and be influenced by, the rest of the design. The discussion of analysis is often the weakest part of a qualitative proposal.

One of the commonest problems in qualitative studies is letting your unanalyzed fieldnotes and transcripts pile up, making the task of final analysis much more difficult and discouraging. There is a mountaineer's adage that the experienced climber begins lunch immediately after finishing breakfast and continues eating lunch as long as he or she is awake, stopping briefly to eat dinner (Manning, 1960). In the same way, the experienced qualitative researcher begins data analysis immediately after finishing the first interview or observation and continues to analyze the data as long as he or she is working on the research, stopping briefly to write reports and papers. Heinrich's (1984) rationale for immediately analyzing his biological data applies equally to the social sciences:

> On a research project I usually try to graph my data on the same day I collect them. From day to day the points on the graph tell me about my progress. It's like a fox pursuing a hare. The graph is the hare's track, and I must stay close to that hare. I have to be able to react and change course frequently. Also, since nature is complex I let it lead me, trying not to get too far ahead, so that I don't have to backtrack. (p. 71)

Seidman (1991, p. 86) states a minority view; he prefers to wait until he's completed all of his interviews before beginning analysis, to avoid having his reading of earlier interviews bias the later ones. For some kinds of studies—ones in which the research questions are well-formulated in advance, interviews or observations are tape-recorded, comparability of interviews or observations is important, and there is little need to allow for flexibility of design—this strategy may be appropriate, but I strongly recommend against this in general. The possible risks of beginning analysis immediately are far outweighed by the advantages of being able to progressively focus your interviews and gain what Glaser (1978) calls *theoretical sensitivity.*

STRATEGIES FOR
QUALITATIVE DATA ANALYSIS

Data analysis is probably the aspect of qualitative research that most clearly distinguishes it from experimental and survey research, and the one that is least familiar to researchers coming to qualitative research from other traditions. As with data collection methods, the following discussion is not intended to explain how to *do* qualitative data analysis; instead, I provide some guidelines for *selecting* data analysis strategies and techniques. I will begin with an overview of qualitative analysis and then discuss some specific issues in making decisions about analytic methods.[5]

The initial step in qualitative analysis is reading the interview transcripts, observational notes, or documents that are to be analyzed (Dey, 1993; Smith, 1979; Tesch, 1990, p. 90). Listening to interview tapes prior to transcription is also an opportunity for analysis, as is the actual process of transcribing interviews or of rewriting and reorganizing your rough observation notes. During this reading or listening, you should write notes and memos on what you see or hear in your data and develop tentative ideas about categories and relationships.

At this point, you have a number of analytic options. These fall into three main groups: memos, categorizing strategies (such as coding and thematic analysis), and contextualizing strategies (such as narrative analysis, individual case studies, and ethnographic microanalysis). These methods can, and generally should, be combined, but I will begin by discussing them separately.

As discussed in Chapter 1, memos can perform other functions not related to data analysis, such as reflection on methods, theory, or purposes; however, they are also an essential technique for qualitative analysis (Miles & Huberman, 1994, pp. 72-75; Strauss & Corbin, 1990, pp. 197-223). You should regularly write memos while you are doing data analysis; memos not only capture your analytic thinking about your data, they *facilitate* such thinking, stimulating analytic insights.

The main categorizing strategy in qualitative research is coding. This is rather different from coding in quantitative research, which consists of applying a preestablished set of categories to the data according to explicit, unambiguous rules, with the primary goal being to generate frequency counts of the items in each category. In qualitative research, in contrast, the goal of coding is not to produce counts of things, but to "fracture" (Strauss, 1987, p. 29) the data and rearrange it into categories that facilitate the comparison of data within and between these categories and that aid in the development of theoretical concepts. Another form of categorizing analysis involves sorting the data into broader themes and issues.

Although some coding categories may be drawn from existing theory, others are developed inductively by the researcher during the analysis, and still others (what are often called *emic* categories) are taken from the conceptual structure of the people studied. The key feature of most qualitative coding is that it is grounded in the data (Glaser & Strauss, 1967); that is, it is developed in interaction with, and is tailored to the understanding of, the particular data being analyzed. Thus, you should keep codes (and memos) linked, either physically or by cross-referencing, to the data that gave rise to them, in order not to lose the original context from which they developed, a problem often called *context stripping*.

What I call *contextualizing strategies* (Maxwell & Miller, 1996; Dey, 1993, refers to these as *linking data*) operate quite differently from categorizing ones such as coding. Instead of fracturing the initial text into discrete elements and re-sorting it into categories, contextualizing analysis attempts to understand the data (usually, but not necessarily, an interview transcript or other textual material) in context, using various methods to identify the relationships among the different elements of the text (Atkinson, 1992; Mishler, 1986). Examples of contextualizing strategies include some types of case studies (Patton, 1990), profiles (Seidman, 1991), some types of discourse analysis (Gee, Michaels, & O'Connor, 1992) and narrative analysis (Connolly & Clandinin, 1990), reading for "voice" (Brown, 1988), and ethnographic microanalysis (Erickson, 1992). What all of these strategies have in common is that they do not focus primarily on relationships of similarity that can be used to sort data into categories independently of context but instead look for relationships that connect statements and events within a context into a coherent whole.

The identification of connections between categories and themes can also be seen as a contextualizing step in analysis (Dey, 1993), but a broader one that works with the results of a prior categorizing analysis. This step is necessary for building theory, a primary goal of analysis. However, it cannot recover the contextual ties that were lost in the original categorizing analysis. A purely contextualizing analysis, on the other hand, is limited to understanding particular individuals or situations and cannot develop a more general theory of what's going on. The two strategies need one another to provide a well-rounded account (Maxwell & Miller, 1996).

Displays constitute an additional analytic strategy; these include matrices or tables, networks or concept maps, and various other forms. They are similar to memos in that they make ideas and analysis visible and permanent and facilitate your thinking about relationships. In data analysis, they

---

EXAMPLE 5.2

A Mismatch Between Questions and Analysis

Mike Agar (1991) was once asked by a foundation to review a report on an interview study they had commissioned of how historians worked. The researchers had used the computer program *The Ethnograph* to code the interviews by topic and collect together all the segments on the same topic; the report discussed each of these common topics and provided examples of how the historians talked about these. However, the foundation felt that the report hadn't really answered their questions, which had to do with how individual historians thought about their work—their own theories about how the different topics were connected and the relationships they saw between their thinking, actions, and results.

Answering the latter question would have required a contextualizing analysis that elucidated these connections in each historian's interview. However, the categorizing analysis on which the report was based fragmented these connections, destroying the contextual unity of each historian's views and allowing only a collective presentation of shared concerns. Agar (1991) argues that the fault was not with *The Ethnograph*, which is extremely useful for answering questions that require categorization, but with its misapplication. He comments that "The Ethnograph represents a *part of* an ethnographic research process. When the part is taken for the whole, you get a pathological metonym that can lead you straight to the right answer to the wrong question" (p. 181).

---

serve two other key functions as well: data reduction and the presentation of data or analysis in a form that allows it to be grasped as a whole. This type of analytic tool has been given its most detailed presentation by Miles and Huberman (1994), but it is employed less systematically and explicitly by many other researchers (e.g., Strauss, 1987).

The distinction between categorizing and contextualizing strategies has important consequences for your overall design. A research question that asks about the way events in a specific context are connected cannot be answered by an exclusively categorizing analytic strategy (see Example 5.2). Conversely, a question about similarities and differences across settings or individuals cannot be answered by an exclusively contextualizing strategy. Your analysis strategies have to be compatible with the questions you are asking.

This distinction also has important implications for the use of computers for data analysis. Although there are now a substantial number of programs available for analyzing qualitative data, almost all of them are primarily designed for coding data and may distort your study toward categorizing, variance-theory approaches (Agar, 1991; Maxwell & Miller, 1996; Example 5.2 illustrates this problem). The development of strategies that explicitly integrate categorizing and contextualizing analysis is still in its infancy; one of the best has been called *composite sequence analysis* (Huberman, 1989/1993; Miles & Huberman, 1994, pp. 204-206). The most detailed discussion of the two strategies is by Dey, 1993.

LINKING METHODS AND QUESTIONS

An essential consideration in designing the methods for your study is that you create a *coherent* design, one in which the different methods fit together compatibly and in which they are integrated with the other components of your design. The most critical connection is with your research questions, but, as discussed above, this is primarily an empirical connection, not just a logical one; if your methods won't provide you with the data you need to answer your questions, you need to change either your questions or methods.

A useful tool in determining this compatibility is a matrix in which you list your questions and identify how each of the components of your methods will help you to get the data to answer these questions. In other words, the matrix displays the justification for your methods decisions. I have included one example of how such a matrix can be used[6] (Table 5.1); such a matrix can be valuable as an appendix to a research proposal. Exercise 5.2 helps you to develop a matrix for your own study.

EXERCISE 5.1
Reflecting on Your Research Relationships

Basically, this exercise is to write a memo reflecting on how you plan to contact the people with whom you are doing your research, how you will present yourself and your research, and what arrangements you expect to negotiate for doing the research and reporting your results; how you think you will be perceived by these people; and what the research, ethical, and personal implications of this process are. The following questions are ones you should keep in mind as you work on this memo:

1. What kind of relationships have you established, or do you plan to establish, with the people whom you are studying? What consequences do you think these will

TABLE 5.1.

Data-Planning Matrix for a Study of American Indian At-Risk High School Students[a]

What do I need to know?	Why do I need to know this?	What kind of data will answer the questions?	Where can I find the data?	Whom do I contact for access?	Time lines for acquisition
What are the truancy rates for American Indian students?	To assess the impact of attendance on American Indian students' persistence in school	Computerized student attendance records	Attendance offices assistant principal's offices for all schools	Mr. Joe Smith, high school assistant principal; Dr. Amanda Jones, middle school principal	August: Establish student database October: Update June: Final tally
What is the academic achievement of the students in the study?	To assess the impact of academic performance on American Indian students' persistence in school	Norm- and criterion-referenced test scores; grades on teacher-made tests; grades on report cards; student portfolios	Counseling offices	High school and middle school counselors; classroom teachers	Compilation #1: End of semester Compilation #2: End of school year
What is the English-language proficiency of the students?	To assess the relationship between language proficiency, academic performance, and persistence in school	Language-assessment test scores; classroom teacher attitude surveys; ESL class grades	Counseling offices; ESL teachers' offices	Counselors' test records; classroom teachers	Collect test scores Sept. 15 Teacher survey, Oct. 10-15 ESL class grades, end of fall semester and end of school year
What do American Indian students dislike about school?	To discover what factors lead to antischool attitudes among American Indian students	Formal and informal student interviews; student survey	Homeroom classes; meetings with individual students	Principals of high school and middle schools; parents of students; homeroom teachers	Obtain student and parent consent forms, Aug.-Sept. Student interviews, Oct.-May 30 Student survey, first week in May

What do students plan to do after high school?	To assess the degree to which coherent post-high school career planning affects high school completion	Student survey; follow-up survey of students attending college and getting jobs	Counseling offices; Tribal Social Services office; Dept. of Probation; Alumni Association	Homeroom teachers; school personnel; parents; former students; community social service workers	Student survey, first week in May Follow-up survey, summer and fall
What do teachers think about their students' capabilities?	To assess teacher expectations of student success	Teacher survey; teacher interviews	—	Building principals; individual classroom teachers	Teacher interviews, November (subgroup) Teacher survey, April (all teachers)
What do teachers know about the home culture of their students?	To assess teachers' cultural awareness	Teacher interviews; teacher survey; logs of participation in staff development activities	Individual teachers' classrooms and records	Building principals; individual classroom teachers; assistant superintendent for staff development	Teacher interviews, November (subgroup) Teacher survey, April (all teachers)
What do teachers do to integrate knowledge of the student's home culture community into their teaching?	To assess the degree of discontinuity between school culture and home culture	Teachers' lesson plans; classroom observations; logs of participation in staff development activities	Individual teachers' classrooms and records	Building principals; individual classroom teachers; assistant superintendent for staff development	Lesson plans, December-June Observations, Sept. 1- May 30 Staff development, June logs

Adapted from LeCompte and Preissle, 1993.
a. Research problem: To what extent do various at-risk conditions contribute to dropping out for American Indian students?

have for your study? What alternative kinds of relationships could you create, and what advantages and disadvantages would these have?

2. How do you think you will be perceived by the people you interact with in your research? How will this affect your relations with these people? What could you do to better understand and modify this perception?

3. What explicit agreements do you plan to negotiate about how the research will be conducted and how you will report the results to the people you are working with? What *implicit* understandings about these issues do you think these people (and you) will have? How will both the implicit and explicit terms of the study affect your research? Do any of these need to be discussed or changed?

4. What ethical issues or problems do these considerations raise? How do you plan to deal with these?

As with the memo on research questions (Exercise 4.1), this can be a valuable memo to discuss with colleagues or fellow students.

EXERCISE 5.2
Questions and Methods Matrix

This exercise has two purposes. The first is for you to link up your research questions and your research methods—to display the logical connections between your research questions and your sampling, data collection, and data analysis decisions. The second purpose is to gain experience using matrices as a tool; matrices are useful not only for research design, but also for ongoing monitoring of sampling and data collection (see Miles & Huberman, 1994, p. 94ff.) and for data analysis.

Doing this exercise can't be a mechanical process; it requires thinking about *how* your methods can provide answers to your research questions. One way to do this is to start with your questions and ask what data you would need, how you can get them, and how you would have to analyze them, in order to answer these questions. You can also work in the other direction: Ask yourself why you want to collect and analyze the data in the way you propose—what will you learn from this? Then examine these connections between your research questions and your methods and work on displaying these connections in a matrix. Doing this may require you to revise your questions or your planned methods, or both. Keep in mind that this exercise is intended to help you make your methods decisions and is not a final formulation of these.

The exercise has two parts:

1. Construct the matrix itself. Your matrix should include columns for research questions, sampling decisions, data collection methods, and kinds of analysis, but you can add any other columns you think would be useful in explaining the logic of your design.

2. Write a brief narrative justification for the choices you make in the matrix. One way to do this is as a separate discussion, by question, of the rationale for your

choices in each row; another way is to include this as a column in the matrix itself (as in Table 5.1).

NOTES

1. This is simply another application of the variance versus process distinction discussed earlier. Rather than just asking about the *degree* of prestructuring and its consequences (treating prestructuring as a variable that can affect other variables), I am concerned with the *ways* that prestructuring is employed in actual studies and how it affects other aspects of the design.

2. John Watkins (personal communication) has called this the *dummy variable* view of the researcher's relationship to the setting and people studied; it's either zero or one.

3. However, he also dismisses one widely used argument for the generalizability of data from a convenience sample—a similarity between some demographic characteristics of the sample and of the population as a whole—as an invalid one.

4. Strauss (1987; Strauss & Corbin, 1990) has developed a strategy that he calls *theoretical sampling*, which is a variation on this third approach. Theoretical sampling is driven by the theory that is inductively developed during the research (rather than by prior theory); it selects for examination those particular settings, individuals, events, or processes that are most relevant to the emerging theory.

5. More detailed discussions of qualitative data analysis can be found in Bogdan and Biklen (1992, Chapter 5), Miles and Huberman (1994), Strauss and Corbin (1990), Weiss (1994, Chapter 6), Tesch (1990), Dey (1993), and Maxwell and Miller (1996).

6. There are numerous examples of other types of matrices in Miles and Huberman (1994).

6

Validity:
How Might You Be Wrong?

In the movie *E.T.: The Extraterrestrial,* there is a scene near the end of the film where the boys and E.T., fleeing from the adults who are trying to capture E.T., suddenly arrive at a clearing and see E.T.'s spaceship hovering overhead. After their initial relief, one of the boys asks, "How's he gonna get up there?" Another answers, "Can't he just beam up?" An older boy gives him a condescending look and replies, "This is the real world."

Validity, like getting to E.T.'s spaceship, is the final component of your design. And as with E.T.'s dilemma, there is no way to "beam up" to valid conclusions. This is the real world. The validity of your results is not guaranteed by following some prescribed procedure. As Brinberg and McGrath (1985) put it, "Validity is not a commodity that can be purchased with techniques" (p. 13). Instead, it depends on the relationship of your conclusions to the real world, and there are no methods that can assure you that you have adequately grasped those aspects of the world that you are studying.

The view that methods could guarantee validity was characteristic of early forms of positivism, which held that scientific knowledge could ultimately be reduced to a logical system that was securely grounded in irrefutable sense data. This position has been largely abandoned by philosophers, and methodologists are also becoming increasingly aware of the problems that this view creates. Validity is a goal rather than a product; it is never something that can be proven or taken for granted. Validity is also relative: it has to be assessed in relationship to the purposes and circumstances of the research, rather than being a context-independent property of methods or conclusions (Maxwell, 1992). Finally, validity threats are made implausible by *evidence,* not methods; methods are only a way of getting evidence that can help you rule out these threats.

This view that validity can't be assimilated to methods is one of the two main reasons that, in the model presented here, I have made validity a distinct component of qualitative design, separate from methods. The second reason is pragmatic: Validity is generally acknowledged to be a key *issue* in research design, and I think it's important that it be explicitly addressed. Przeworski and Salomon (1988) identify, as one of three questions proposal readers seek answers to, "How will we know that the conclusions are valid?" And Bosk (1979), in a study of the professional training of surgeons, states that "all fieldwork done by a single field worker invites the question, Why should we believe it?" (p. 193). A lack of explicit attention to validity threats is a common reason for the rejection of research proposals. Making validity a formal component of design can help you to address this issue.

THE CONCEPT OF VALIDITY

In this book, I use validity in a fairly straightforward, commonsense way to refer to the correctness or credibility of a description, conclusion, explanation, interpretation, or other sort of account. I think that this commonsense use of the term is consistent with the way it is generally used by qualitative researchers, and it does not pose any serious philosophical problems.[1] This use of the term "validity" does not imply the existence of any objective truth to which an account can be compared. However, the idea of objective truth isn't essential to a theory of validity that does what most researchers want it to do, which is to give them some grounds for distinguishing accounts that are credible from those that are not. Nor are you required to attain some ultimate truth in order for your study to be useful and believable.

Geertz (1973) tells the story of a British gentleman in colonial India who, upon hearing that the world rested on the backs of four elephants, who in turn stood on the back of a giant turtle, asked what the turtle stood on. Another turtle. And that turtle? "Ah, Sahib, after that it is turtles all the way down" (p. 29). Geertz's point is that there is no "bottom turtle" of ethnographic interpretation, that cultural analysis is essentially incomplete. Although I accept Geertz's point, I would emphasize a different lesson: that you do not have to get to the bottom turtle to have a valid conclusion. You only have to get to a turtle you can stand on securely.

As Campbell (1988), Putnam (1990), and others have argued, we don't need an observer-independent "gold standard" to which we can compare our accounts to see if they are valid. All we require is the possibility of *testing* these accounts against the world, giving the phenomena that we are trying to understand the chance to prove us wrong. The key concept for validity is thus the validity *threat*: a way you might be wrong. These threats are often conceptualized as alternative explanations, or what Huck and Sandler (1979) call *rival hypotheses*. Validity, as a component of your research design, consists of the strategies you use to rule out these threats.

There are important differences between quantitative and qualitative designs in the ways they typically deal with validity threats. Quantitative and experimental researchers generally attempt to design, in advance, controls that will deal with both anticipated and unanticipated threats to validity. These include control groups, statistical control of extraneous variables, randomized sampling and assignment, the framing of explicit hypotheses in advance of collecting the data, and the use of tests of statistical significance. These prior controls deal with most validity threats in an anonymous, generic fashion; as Campbell (1984) puts it, "randomization purports to control an infinite number of 'rival hypotheses' *without specifying what any of them are*" (p. 8).

Qualitative researchers, on the other hand, rarely have the benefit of formal comparisons, sampling strategies, or statistical manipulations that "control for" the effect of particular variables, and they must try to rule out most validity threats after the research has begun, using evidence collected during the research itself to make these alternative hypotheses implausible. This strategy of addressing particular validity threats *after* a tentative account has been developed, rather than attempting to eliminate such threats through prior features of the research design, is in fact more fundamental to scientific method than is the latter approach (Campbell, 1988; Platt, 1964). However, this approach requires you to identify the *specific* threat in question and to develop ways to attempt to rule out that particular threat.

This conception of validity threats and how they can be dealt with is a key issue in a qualitative research proposal. Many proposal writers make the mistake of talking about validity only in general, theoretical terms, presenting abstract strategies such as bracketing, member checks, and triangulation that will supposedly protect their studies from invalidity. In qualitative proposals, such presentations often appear to be "boilerplate"— language that has been borrowed from methods books or successful proposals, without any demonstration that the author has thought through how these strategies will actually be applied in the proposed study. These sections of the proposal often remind me of magical charms that are intended to drive away evil; they lack any evidence for how these strategies will work in practice, and their use seems to be based largely on faith in their supernatural powers.

In contrast, the main emphasis of a qualitative proposal ought to be on how you will rule out *particular* plausible alternatives to your interpretations and explanations. Citations of authorities and invocation of standard approaches are less important than providing a clear argument that the approaches described will adequately deal with the particular threats in question, in the context of the study being proposed. Martha Regan-Smith's proposal (Appendix A) provides a good example of such an argument.

TYPES OF VALIDITY
IN QUALITATIVE RESEARCH

In Chapters 2 and 4, I presented a typology of the kinds of understanding that are involved in qualitative research; here, I want to discuss the implications of this typology for validity. (For a more detailed discussion and justification of this typology, see Maxwell, 1992). Each of the three main types of understanding—description, interpretation, and theory—has distinct threats to its validity. Discussion of a fourth type of understanding, generalization, will be deferred until the end of the chapter, because it poses quite different issues for a qualitative study than the previous three types.

Description. The main threat to valid description, in the sense of describing what you saw and heard, is the inaccuracy or incompleteness of the data. The audio or video recording of observations and interviews, and verbatim transcription of these recordings, largely solves this problem; if you are not doing this, it poses a potentially serious threat to the validity of your study. If your description of what you were observing, or of the interview you conducted, is invalid, then any interpretations or conclusions you draw from these descriptions are questionable. For this reason, you should *always* record and transcribe interviews unless there is a strong reason not to. If lack of time or resources for transcribing is an issue, recording is still preferable to not recording; you can always listen to the tapes. For observation, recording is both more difficult to do and more trouble to transcribe, but it should always be considered as an option; if you do not videotape, you need to make your observational notes as detailed, concrete, and chronological as possible.

Interpretation. The main threat to valid interpretation is imposing one's own framework or meaning, rather than understanding the perspective of the people studied and the meanings they attach to their words and actions. There are several ways that this happens: not listening for the participants' meanings; not being aware of and bracketing your own framework and assumptions; asking leading, closed, or short-answer questions that don't give participants the opportunity to reveal their own perspective. The most important check on such validity threats is to seriously and systematically attempt to learn how the participants in your study make sense of what's going on, rather than pigeonholing their words and actions in your own framework. The strategy known as *member checks*, discussed below, is one of the main ways of avoiding this threat.

Theory. The most serious threat to the theoretical validity of an account is not collecting or paying attention to discrepant data, or not considering alternative explanations or understandings of the phenomena you are studying (cf. Lave & March, 1975). Pelto and Pelto (1978, pp. 25-26) argue that a key problem in anthropological research is the establishment of vague and abstract propositions through anecdotal evidence, without consideration of what could disprove these propositions; they claim that this is the main reason that the personal values of the anthropologist have been so influential.

TWO SPECIFIC VALIDITY THREATS: BIAS AND REACTIVITY

I have argued that qualitative researchers generally deal with validity threats as particular events or processes that could lead to invalid conclusions, rather than as generic variables that need to be controlled. It clearly would be impossible for me to list all, or even the most important, validity threats to the conclusions of a qualitative study, as Cook and Campbell (1979) attempt to do for quasi-experimental studies. What I want to do here, instead, is to discuss two broad types of threats to validity that are often raised in relation to qualitative studies: researcher bias, and the effect of the research on the setting or individuals studied, generally known as reactivity.

Researcher Bias

Two important threats to the validity of qualitative conclusions are the selection of data that fit the researcher's existing theory or preconceptions and the selection of data that "stand out" to the researcher (Miles & Huberman,

1994, p. 263; Shweder, 1980). However, it is clearly impossible to deal with these problems by eliminating the researcher's theories, preconceptions, or values, as discussed in Chapters 2 and 3; this impossibility is one aspect of what has been called the inherent *reflexivity* (Hammersley & Atkinson, 1983) of qualitative research. Nor is it usually appropriate to try to standardize the researcher to achieve reliability; qualitative research is not primarily concerned with eliminating variance between researchers in the values and expectations they bring to the study, but with understanding how a particular researcher's values influence the conduct and conclusions of the study. Explaining your possible biases and how you will deal with these is a key task of your research proposal. As one qualitative researcher, Fred Hess (personal communication), has phrased it, validity in qualitative research is not the result of indifference, but of integrity.

Reactivity

The influence of the researcher on the setting or individuals studied, a problem generally known as *reactivity,* is a second problem that is often raised about qualitative studies. The approach to reactivity of most quantitative research, of trying to control for the effect of the researcher, is appropriate to a variance theory perspective, in which the goal is to prevent researcher variability from being an unwanted cause of variability in the outcome variables. However, eliminating the *actual* influence of the researcher is impossible (Hammersley & Atkinson, 1983), and the goal in a qualitative study is not to eliminate this influence but to understand it and to use it productively.

For participant observation studies, reactivity is generally not as serious a validity threat as some people believe. Becker (1970) points out that in natural settings, an observer is generally much less of an influence on participants' behavior than is the setting itself (although there are clearly exceptions to this, such as situations in which illegal behavior occurs). For interviews, in contrast, reactivity is a powerful and inescapable influence; what the informant says is *always* a function of the interviewer and the interview situation. Although there are some things you can do to prevent the more undesirable consequences of this, such as avoiding leading questions, trying to minimize your effect is not a meaningful goal for qualitative research. As discussed above for bias, what is important is to understand *how* you are influencing what the informant says, and how this affects the validity of the inferences you can draw from the interview (cf. Briggs, 1986; Mishler, 1986).

VALIDITY TESTS: A CHECKLIST

Although methods and procedures do not guarantee validity, they are nonetheless essential to the process of ruling out validity threats and increasing the credibility of your conclusions. For this reason, I provide below a checklist of some of the most important strategies that can be used for this purpose. Miles and Huberman (1994, pp. 262ff.) include a more extensive list, some of which overlaps with mine, and other lists are given by Becker (1970), Kidder (1981), Guba and Lincoln (1989), and Patton (1990). What follows is not a compilation of what these authors say—I strongly urge you to consult their discussions—but simply my own list of what I see as most important.

The overall point I want to make about these strategies is that they primarily operate not by *verifying* conclusions, but by *testing* the validity of your conclusions and the existence of potential threats to those conclusions (Campbell, 1988). The fundamental process in all of these tests is trying to finding evidence that challenges your conclusion, or that makes the potential threat implausible.

Keep in mind that these strategies are effective only if you actually use them. Simply invoking them as magical spells won't drive the validity threats away. Nor will putting them in your proposal as boilerplate convince most reviewers; you will need to demonstrate that you have thought through how you can effectively use them in your own study.

1. The Modus Operandi (MO) Approach

One strategy often used for testing qualitative conclusions has been called the *modus operandi* method by Scriven (1974). It resembles the approach of a detective trying to solve a crime, an FAA inspector trying to determine the cause of an airplane crash, a physician attempting to diagnose a patient's illness, or a historian, geologist, or evolutionary biologist trying to account for a particular sequence of events. However, its logic has received little formal explication (recent exceptions are Gould, 1989; Mohr, 1982; Ragin, 1987), and it has not been clearly understood even by many qualitative researchers. Basically, rather than trying to control for validity threats as variables, by holding them constant in some fashion, the modus operandi method deals with them as *events,* by searching for clues as to whether or not they took place and were involved in the phenomenon in question.

The major problem in using the MO approach in qualitative research is the difficulty of generating an adequate list of alternative plausible explanations or interpretations that need to be ruled out; often, this requires the help of others who have some distance from the study (Miles & Huberman, 1994, p. 275). This is one reason that validity testing in qualitative research can't be reduced to a mechanical procedure. A list of some of the main types of validity threats can be helpful, and I have tried to provide some of these above, but ultimately the identification of plausible validity threats requires a creative and open-ended approach, rather than simply going through a preestablished checklist such as that given by Campbell and Stanley (1963).

A second reason that this process can't be reduced to an algorithm is that the identification of something as a validity threat is theory-dependent. This is generally acknowledged to be true in all science, and qualitative research is no exception. The recognition of alternative interpretations and explanations is influenced by the theory that you hold of the phenomenon being studied—what you see as relevant. Miles and Huberman (1994, p. 275) warn that you should avoid premature decisions about what counts as a possible validity threat and keep your list of threats open.

2. Searching for Discrepant Evidence and Negative Cases

Identifying and analyzing discrepant data and negative cases is a key part of the attempt to falsify a proposed conclusion. Instances that cannot be accounted for by a particular interpretation or explanation can point up important defects in that account. However, there are times when an apparently discrepant instance is not persuasive, as when the interpretation of the discrepant data is itself in doubt. Physics is full of examples of supposedly disconfirming experimental evidence that was later found to be flawed. The basic principle here is that you need to rigorously examine both the supporting and discrepant data to assess whether it is more plausible to retain or modify the conclusion, being aware of all of the pressures to ignore data that do not fit your conclusions. In particularly difficult cases, the best you may be able to do is to report the discrepant evidence and allow readers to evaluate this and draw their own conclusions (Wolcott, 1990).

3. Triangulation

Triangulation—collecting information from a diverse range of individuals and settings, using a variety of methods—was discussed in Chapter 5. This strategy reduces the risk of chance associations and of systematic biases due to a specific method and allows a better assessment of the generality of the explanations that you develop. The most extensive discussion of triangulation as a validity-testing strategy in qualitative research is by Fielding and Fielding (1986).

One of Fielding and Fielding's key points is that it is not true that triangulation automatically increases validity. First, the methods that are triangulated may have the *same* biases and sources of invalidity, thus providing only a false sense of security. For example, interviews, questionnaires, and documents are all vulnerable to self-report bias. Second, the researcher may consciously or unconsciously select those methods or data sources that would tend to support the preferred conclusions.

Fielding and Fielding (1986) thus emphasize the need to recognize the fallibility of *any* particular method or data and to triangulate in terms of validity threats. As argued above, you should think about what particular sources of error or bias might exist and look for specific ways to deal with this, rather than relying on your selection of methods to do this for you.

4. Feedback

Soliciting feedback from others is an extremely useful strategy for identifying validity threats, your own biases and assumptions, and flaws in your logic or methods. Consistent with the philosophy underlying triangulation, you should try to get such feedback from a variety of people, both those familiar with the phenomena or settings you're studying and those who are strangers to this situation. They will give you different sorts of comments, but both are valuable.

5. Member Checks

One particular sort of feedback deserves special attention. This is systematically soliciting feedback about one's data and conclusions from the people you are studying, a process known as member checks (Guba & Lincoln, 1989). It is the single most important way of ruling out the possibility of misinterpretation of the meaning of what they say and the perspective they have on what is going on. However, Bloor (1983) argues that such validation strategies are more problematic than most researchers seem to believe. It is important not to assume that the participants' pronouncements are necessarily valid; their responses should be taken simply as evidence regarding the validity of your account (cf. Hammersley & Atkinson, 1983). For a more detailed discussion of this strategy, see Miles and Huberman (1984, pp. 242-243) and Guba and Lincoln (1989).

6. "Rich" Data

By "rich" data, I mean data that are detailed and complete enough that they provide a full and revealing picture of what is going on.[2] In interview studies, such data generally require verbatim transcripts of the interviews, rather than simply notes on what you noticed or felt was significant. For observation, rich data are the product of detailed, descriptive note taking about the specific, concrete events that you observe. Becker (1970) argues that such data

> counter the twin dangers of respondent duplicity and observer bias by making it difficult for respondents to produce data that uniformly support a mistaken conclusion, just as they make it difficult for the observer to restrict his observations so that he sees only what supports his prejudices and expectations. (p. 53)

In both cases, the key function of rich data is to provide a *test* of one's developing theories, rather than simply a *source* of supporting instances.

7. Quasi-Statistics

Many of the conclusions of qualitative studies have an implicit quantitative component. Any claim that a particular phenomenon is typical, rare, or prevalent in the setting or population studied is an inherently quantitative claim and requires some quantitative support. Becker (1970) has coined the term *quasi-statistics* to refer to the use of simple numerical results that can be readily derived from the data. He argues that "one of the greatest faults in most observational case studies has been their failure to make explicit the quasi-statistical basis of their conclusions" (pp. 81-82).

Quasi-statistics not only allow you to test and support claims that are inherently quantitative, but also enable you to assess the *amount* of evidence in your data that bears on a particular conclusion or threat, such as how many discrepant instances exist and from how many different sources they were obtained. This strategy is used effectively in a classic participant-observation study of medical students by Becker et al. (1961/1977), which presents over 50 tables and graphs of the amount and distribution of observational and interview data supporting their conclusions.

8. Comparison

Although explicit comparisons (such as control groups) for the purpose of assessing validity threats are mainly associated with quantitative, variance-theory research, there are valid uses for comparison in qualitative studies, particularly multisite studies (e.g., Miles & Huberman, 1984, p. 237). In addition, single case studies often incorporate implicit comparisons that contribute to the interpretability of the case. There may be a literature on typical settings of the type studied that make it easier to identify the relevant factors in an exceptional case and ascertain their importance. In other instances, the participants in the setting studied may themselves have experience with other settings or with the same setting at an earlier time, and the researcher may be able to draw on this experience to identify the crucial factors and the effect that these have.

For example, Martha Regan-Smith's (1992) study of medical school teaching and its effect on student learning (Appendix A) included only faculty who had won the Best Teacher award; from the point of view of quantitative design, this was an "uncontrolled" study, vulnerable to all of the validity threats identified by Campbell and Stanley (1963). However, both of the previously mentioned forms of implicit comparison were employed in the research. First, there is a great deal of published information about medical school teaching, and Regan-Smith was able to use both this background and her own extensive knowledge of medical schools to identify what was distinctive about the teachers she studied. Second, the students she interviewed explicitly contrasted these teachers with others whose classes they felt were not as helpful to them. In addition to these comparisons, the validity of her research conclusions depended substantially on a process approach; the students explained in detail not only what it was that the exemplary teachers did that increased their learning, but how and why these teaching methods were beneficial. Many of these explanations were corroborated by Regan-Smith's own experiences as a participant-observer in these teachers' classes and by the teachers' explanations of why they taught the way they did.

GENERALIZATION IN QUALITATIVE RESEARCH

I have deliberately left generalization until the end, because I consider it a separate issue from validity proper. Qualitative researchers usually study a single setting or a small number of individuals or sites, using theoretical or purposive rather than probability sampling, and they rarely make explicit claims about the generalizability of their accounts. However, it is important to distinguish between what I call *internal* and *external* generalizability (Maxwell, 1992). Internal generalizability refers to the generalizability of a conclusion *within* the setting or group studied, whereas external generalizability refers to its generalizability beyond that setting or group. Internal generalizability is clearly a key issue for qualitative case studies; it corresponds to what Cook and Campbell (1979) call *statistical conclusion validity* in quantitative research. The descriptive, interpretive, and theoretical validity of the conclusions all depend on their internal generalizability to the case as a whole. If you are studying the patterns of interaction between the teacher and students in a single classroom, your account of that classroom as a whole is seriously jeopardized if you have selectively focused on particular students or kinds of interactions and ignored others.

In contrast, external generalizability is often not a crucial issue for qualitative studies. Indeed, the value of a qualitative study may depend on its *lack* of external generalizability, in the sense of being representative of a larger population; it may provide an account of a setting or population that is illuminating as an extreme case or ideal type. Eliot Freidson, for his study of social control among physicians (Example 3.2), selected an atypical group practice, one which was staffed by physicians who were better trained and whose views were more progressive than usual, and which was structured precisely to deal with the issues he was addressing. He argues that his study makes an important contribution to theory and policy precisely because this was a group for whom social controls on practice should have been most likely to be effective. The failure of such controls in this case not only highlights a social process that is likely to exist in other groups, but also provides a more persuasive argument for the unworkability of such controls than would a study of a representative group.

This does not mean that qualitative studies are never generalizable beyond the setting or informants studied. First, qualitative studies often have what Judith Singer (personal communication) has called *face generalizability;* there is no obvious reason *not* to believe that the results apply more generally. Second, the generalizability of qualitative studies usually is based, not on explicit sampling of some defined population to which the results can be extended, but on the development of a theory that can be extended to other cases (Becker, 1991; Ragin, 1987; Yin, 1994). Third, Hammersley (1992, pp. 189-191) and Weiss (1994, pp. 26-29) list a number of features that lend plausibility to generalizations from case studies or nonrandom samples, including respondents' own assessments of generalizability, the similarity of dynamics and constraints to other situations, the presumed depth or universality of the phenomenon studied, and corroboration from other studies. All of these characteristics can provide credibility to generalizations from qualitative studies, but none permit the kinds of precise extrapolation of results to defined populations that probability sampling allows.

EXERCISE 6.1
Dealing With Validity Threats to Your Study

1. What are the most serious validity threats (alternative explanations) that you need to be concerned with in your study? In other words, what are the main ways in which you might be mistaken about what's going on? Be as specific as you can, rather than just giving general categories. Also, think about *why* you think these might be serious threats.

2. What could you do in your research design (including data collection and data analysis) to deal with these threats and increase the credibility of your conclusions? Start by brainstorming possible solutions, and then consider which of these strategies are *practical* for your study, as well as theoretically relevant.

Remember that some validity threats are unavoidable; you will need to acknowledge these in your proposal or in the conclusions to your study, but no one expects you to have airtight answers to *every* possible threat. The key issue is how plausible and how serious these unavoidable threats are.

NOTES

1. For the philosophical argument that informs these statements, see Maxwell (1992).

2. Some qualitative researchers refer to this sort of data as *thick description,* a phrase coined by the philosopher Gilbert Ryle (1949) and applied to ethnographic research by Clifford Geertz (1973). However, this is not what Ryle and Geertz meant by the phrase. Thick description, as Geertz uses it, is description that incorporates the intentions of the actors and the codes of signification that give the actions meaning for them, what anthropologists call an *emic* account. It has nothing to do with the amount of detail provided. (For a more detailed discussion of this issue, see Maxwell, 1992, pp. 288-289.)

7

Research Proposals: Presenting and Justifying a Qualitative Study

The Empress Catherine the Great of Russia once decided to take a cruise down the Danube to view that part of her realm. Her prime minister, Grigori Potemkin, knowing that the poverty of this region would not be pleasing to the Empress, allegedly built fake villages along the banks of the river and forcibly staffed these with cheering peasants, in order to impress the Empress with how prosperous and thriving the area was. The term "Potemkin village" has since come to be used to refer to "an impressive facade or show designed to hide an undesirable fact or condition" (*Merriam-Webster's Collegiate Dictionary*).

Some proposals are to a significant extent Potemkin villages. What is presented does not reflect what the author actually believes or plans to do but is fabricated in order to get approval or money for the study. Such proposals are frequently the result of the writer not having worked out (or worse, not having understood the *need* to work out) the actual design of the study, and thus having to substitute a fake design for this. Aside from the fact that reviewers are usually fairly good at detecting such facades, the most serious danger of a Potemkin village proposal is that you may be taken in by your own fabrication, thinking that you have in fact solved your design problems and ignoring your actual theories, purposes, questions, and situation and the implications of these—your real research design. An ignorance of, or refusal to acknowledge, this real design and the conditions that affect it is certain to get you in trouble when you actually try to do the study.

Of course, as discussed in previous chapters, your research design will evolve as you conduct the study, and therefore a proposal for a qualitative study can't present an exact specification of what you will do. However, this is no excuse for not developing the design for your study in as much detail as you can at this point, or for failing to clearly communicate this design; in your proposal, you simply need to explain the kinds of flexibility that your study requires and to indicate, as best you can, how you will go about making future design decisions. In my experience, a key concern in evaluating qualitative proposals is whether or not the researcher has demonstrated the *ability* to design a coherent and feasible study, providing evidence that he or she is aware of the key issues that will need to be addressed and of the possible strategies for dealing with these.

In this chapter, I want to explain the connections between a study's research design and an effective proposal for that study and to provide some guidelines and advice on how to accomplish the transition from design to proposal. I believe that the model of design I have presented in this book simplifies and facilitates this transition and provides a useful framework for thinking about proposal structure and content. More detailed and specific advice on proposal writing is provided by Locke et al. (1993).

I will begin with the purposes and structure of a research proposal and then take up the ways in which the design of your study connects to these purposes and structure. Finally, I will discuss the specific parts of a proposal and the key issues that a proposal for qualitative research needs to address.

THE PURPOSE OF A PROPOSAL

The structure of a proposal isn't governed by an arbitrary set of rules; it's closely tied to the *purpose* of a proposal. This purpose is so fundamental that when you are working on a proposal you should post it above your desk or computer:

> The purpose of a proposal is to explain and justify your proposed study to an audience of nonexperts on your topic.

There are four key concepts in this statement:

1. *Explain:* You want your readers to clearly understand what you plan to do. Locke et al. (1993) emphasize that "advisers and reviewers misunderstand student proposals far more often than they disagree with what is proposed" (p. 123). This observation is abundantly supported by my own experience, both with advising students and reviewing student proposals, and with submitting and reviewing grant proposals. In writing and editing your proposal, *clarity* is a primary goal.

2. *Justify:* You want the readers of your proposal to understand not only what you plan to do, but *why*—your rationale for doing this. Proposals are often turned down, even when the study is clearly described, because it isn't clear why the author wants to do the study this way. Your readers may not understand how your proposed methods will provide valid answers to your research questions, or how the questions address important issues or purposes. They may also question whether *you* have a good reason for doing the study this way, or are simply using boilerplate language that you've borrowed from other studies.

3. *Your proposed study:* Your proposal should be about *your study,* not the literature, your research topic, or research methods in general. You should ruthlessly edit out anything in the proposal that does not directly contribute to the explanation and justification of your study. A proposal is no place to display your general knowledge of the literature on your topic, your theoretical or methodological sophistication, or your political views on the issues you plan to investigate;[1] this will generally annoy your reviewers, who are trying to determine if your proposed study makes sense.

Students sometimes make the mistake of focusing their proposal on their planned dissertation, rather than on the research that they propose to do. They provide lengthy, chapter-by-chapter descriptions of what the dissertation will cover, using language such as "In my dissertation, I will discuss . . . ." Although it can occasionally be helpful, in explaining and justifying your study, to refer to how you intend to present this in the dissertation, far more often these references to your dissertation are red herrings, interfering with your presentation of the actual research and its design.

4. *Nonexperts:* You can't assume any particular specialized knowledge on the part of your readers. Grant proposals in the social sciences and related fields are generally *not* assigned to readers on the basis of their expertise on your specific topic, and students often will have faculty reviewing their proposals who are not knowledgeable about the specific area of the proposed study. You need to carefully examine your proposal to make sure that everything in it will be clear to a nonspecialist. (The best way to do this is generally to give the proposal to some nonspecialists and ask them to tell you what isn't clear.)

THE PROPOSAL AS AN ARGUMENT

Another way of putting the points made above is that a proposal is an argument *for* your study. It needs to explain the logic behind the proposed study, rather than simply describe or summarize the study, and to do so in a way that nonspecialists will understand. (It should not, however, attempt to defend your anticipated conclusions: doing so is almost certain to raise serious questions about your own biases.) Each piece of your proposal should be a clear answer to a salient question about your study.

The essential feature of a good argument is *coherence,* and a proposal needs to be coherent in two different senses of this term. First, it has to *cohere*—flow logically from one point to the next and hang together as an integrated whole. The connections between different components of your design are crucial to this coherence. You need to understand why you're doing what you are, rather than blindly following rules, models, or standard practice. Without this, you won't be able to give a coherent justification for your design.

Second, it has to *be coherent*—to make sense to the reviewers. You need to put yourself in your readers' shoes, and think about how what you say will be understood by them. Often, a key to writing in a way that will make sense to these readers is avoiding jargon, unnecessarily complex style, and what Becker (1986) calls classy writing. Martha Regan-Smith's (1992) proposal (Appendix A) is an example of clear, straightforward language that avoids these problems.

These two aspects of coherence are the source of the most common problems with proposals: Either they have inconsistencies or gaps in their reasoning, or they don't adequately communicate to the reviewers what the author wants to do and why, or both. These are issues that should be foremost in your mind when you are writing a proposal, because they will be foremost in the minds of those reviewing it.

THE RELATIONSHIP BETWEEN RESEARCH DESIGN AND PROPOSAL ARGUMENT

There are a number of questions that reviewers will be asking in reading your proposal, questions that the argument of your proposal needs to address. Locke et al. (1993) state that

> The author must answer three questions:
> 1. What do we already know or do?
> 2. How does this particular question relate to what we already know or do?
> 3. Why select this particular method of investigation? (p. 18)

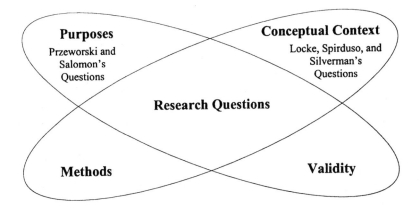

Figure 7.1. Relationship Between Research Design and Questions About Research Proposals

These questions emphasize the connections along one axis of my model of research design: the one that runs from the upper right to lower left of the diagram, consisting of the Conceptual Context, Research Questions, and Methods (see Figure 7.1).

In contrast, Przeworski and Salomon (1988), in their suggestions for applicants seeking funding from the Social Science Research Council, state that

> every proposal reader constantly scans for clear answers to three questions:
>> What are we going to learn as the result of the proposed project that we do not already know?
>> Why is it worth knowing?
>> How will we know that the conclusions are valid? (p. 2)

These questions, in contrast to those of Locke et al., emphasize the connections along the other axis of the model, the one that runs from the upper left to lower right of the diagram, including Purposes, Research Questions, and Validity.

Thus, the relationships among the components of your research design constitute a crucial part of the argument of your proposal. These relationships provide the coherence that your argument depends on. Above all else, your proposal must convey to the readers what these connections are.

THE PROPOSAL AS A LITERARY FORM

In addition, a proposal is like a sonnet, a haiku, or a limerick; it is supposed to have a definite structure, and this structure is a key means for conveying its argument. Not following this structure can get you in trouble:

There was a young man from Japan
Whose limericks no one could scan.
When asked why this was,
He replied, "It's because
I always try to get as many words in the last line as I possibly can."

This is *not* a limerick; it's a parody of a limerick, a joke. It deliberately violates the rule about how many syllables one can have in the last line, and in the process reveals why this young man's limericks were so confusing to his readers.

Although a proposal is not nearly as rigid in its prescribed structure as a haiku or limerick, it is not as open as a novel or short story. Reviewers generally expect a proposal to have one of a number of standard formats, and they tend to become confused or annoyed when proposals fail to meet this expectation. In reading students' proposals, I have sometimes had the same reaction as the readers of the young man's limericks—that the student is "trying to get as many words in the last line as he or she possibly can," having lost sight of the inherent structure of the proposal.

A MODEL FOR PROPOSAL STRUCTURE

The model of research design that I have presented in this book can be directly mapped onto one way of organizing a qualitative proposal. This format is by no means the only way to structure a proposal, but it is a fairly standard and generally understood format, and one which lends itself particularly well to communicating the design of a qualitative study.

DESIGN   **PROPOSAL**

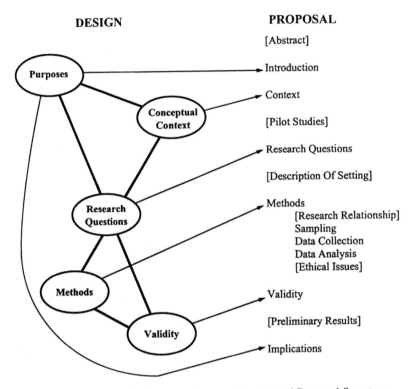

Figure 7.2. Relationship Between Research Design and Proposal Structure

However, every university and funding source has its own requirements and preferences regarding proposal structure, and these must take precedence for your proposal if they conflict with what I present here. I will first display the relationships between research design and proposal structure in diagram form (Figure 7.2) and then go through each part of the proposal structure in detail, explaining how it relates to my model of research design. This explanation will make more sense if it is read in conjunction with Martha Regan-Smith's proposal for a qualitative study of what four outstanding medical school teachers do to help students learn basic science, along with my commentary on this proposal (Appendix A).

1. Abstract

Not all proposals will require an abstract, but if you need to have one, this is the place to provide an overview and "road map," not just of the study itself, but of the argument of your proposal. Your abstract should present in summary form the actual argument for your research, not simply provide placeholders that will later be filled in with real content (Becker, 1986, pp. 50-53). Regan-Smith's (1992) abstract (Appendix A) is a model for how to do this.

2. Introduction

The introduction to your proposal "sets the stage for your research, explaining . . . what you want to do and why" (Peters, 1992, p. 202). It should clearly present the purposes of your study and give a general overview of your main research questions and of the kind of study you are proposing. (A full presentation of your research questions is often better reserved until after the context section, when the theoretical grounding of the questions will be clearer, but this is not an absolute rule.) It should also explain the structure of the proposal itself, if this could be confusing. The introduction should normally be fairly short, about two or three double-spaced pages.

3. Research Context

This section is often called the *literature review,* but this is a misleading term, for reasons that I explained in Chapter 3. The purpose of this section of the proposal is not to review a particular body of literature, but, first, to show how your proposed research fits into what is already known (its relationship to existing theory and research) and how it makes a contribution to our understanding of your topic and, second, to explain the theoretical framework that informs your study. These purposes are usually accomplished by discussing prior theory and research, but the point is not to summarize what's already been done in this field but to ground your proposed study in the relevant previous work and to give the reader a clear sense of your theoretical approach to the phenomena that you propose to study. Although some books on proposal writing argue that your proposal needs to demonstrate your familiarity with the literature in your field, I think this is misleading advice in general. The grain of truth in this view is that you need to deal with those studies, theories, and approaches that your readers may *believe* are relevant to your research, and if you feel that they are not in fact relevant, explain why.[2]

Insofar as your personal experience and knowledge form an important part of your conceptual context, these should be discussed here; Martha Regan-Smith devotes a separate part of her Context section to these. The key issue, again, is relevance; the connection of the experience and views discussed in this section to your study must be clear.

Any pilot studies that you have done also need to be discussed in the proposal and their implications for your research explained. This can be done in any of three places: at the end of the Context section; in a separate section immediately following Context; or, in some cases, after the presentation of your research questions, if a detailed grasp of these questions is important to understanding the pilot studies. Unless an important purpose of the pilot study was to try out the methods that you plan to use in the proposed research, you should focus your discussion of your pilot studies on what you learned from them, rather than on the details of what you did.

If you have already collected a substantial proportion of the data for your study (as is sometimes the case for dissertation proposals), you may want to include a section on your preliminary results, as discussed below. For an example of how this can be done, see the section of Regan-Smith's proposal on preliminary findings.

4. Research Questions

As in my model of research design, the statement of your research questions is the central part of your proposal. Although it is sometimes feasible to present your detailed research questions in the Introduction, it is usually clearer to defer this until after the Context section, because the reasons for focusing on these particular questions may not be apparent until the context of prior research, theory, and experience has been described. This section should usually fall more or less in the middle of the proposal. If it is quite a ways from the middle, this may be a sign that the Context and Methods sections are out of balance with one another, that one is too long and the other too short.

The Research Questions section, in addition to stating your questions, should clarify two key points, if the answers to these are not obvious. First, it should explain how your questions relate to prior research and theory, to your own experience and exploratory research, and to your purposes. Second, it should clarify the overall focus of your questions; how they form a coherent whole, rather than being a random collection of queries about your topic. Generally, a small number of clearly focused questions are far better than a larger number of questions that attempt to "cover the waterfront" on your topic. If you have more than two or three major questions, you need to think about whether some of these are best seen as subquestions of a broader question, or if your study is in fact attempting to do too much.

5. Research Methods[3]

Your proposal probably doesn't need to justify qualitative methods in general, unless you have reasons to think that your reviewers will be ignorant of, or prejudiced against, this approach.[4] You do need to explain and justify the *particular* methods decisions you've made; for every decision, it should be clear why this is a reasonable choice. If you can't specify certain parts of your methods in advance (e.g., how many interviews you'll do), explain the basis on which you'll make your decision.

A description of the setting or social context of your study can be helpful in clarifying and justifying your choice of questions and methods. This description can be placed at the beginning of the Methods section, or it can be a separate section just before or after Research Questions. A proposal for funding will also need to explain what resources you already have and what ones you are requesting money for, your qualifications and experience, and your timetable and budget; some of this can be included in Methods, but you will probably need additional sections as well.[5]

The Methods section normally has several parts:

a. Research design in the narrow sense: what kind of a study is this? This is often not necessary in a qualitative study, but it can sometimes be helpful to describe and justify the overall approach taken; for example, to explain why you have chosen to conduct a case study or a comparison of two settings. If this doesn't require a detailed explanation, it can often be addressed in the Introduction; if your research questions are closely tied to the kind of study you are doing (e.g., if you are comparing two settings and your questions focus on this comparison), this may be best addressed in the section on Research Questions.

b. The research relationship you establish with those you are studying. This is an important part of your design, as argued above, but it is not usually an explicit part of a proposal. My advice is to discuss this relationship, particularly if it is an important and nonobvious source of information or insights, or if it raises potential ethical problems or validity threats for the study.

c. Sampling—your decisions about sources of data, including sites, persons, places, and times. It is important not simply to describe these, but to *justify* them: to explain why you have decided to study these particular settings or to interview this particular selection or number of people.

d. Data collection—how you'll get the information you need to answer your research questions. This should include a description of the kinds of interviews, observations, or other methods you plan to use, how you will conduct these, and why you have chosen these methods. For both sampling and data collection, practical considerations are often important, and your proposal should be candid about these, rather than ignoring them or concocting bogus theoretical justifications for decisions that are practically based. If any of your decisions *are* based mainly on practical considerations (such as studying an institution where you have contacts and easy access), you need to deal at some point with any potential validity threats or ethical risks that this raises.

e. Data analysis—what you'll do to make sense of the data you collect. Be explicit about how your data will be analyzed; specific examples are generally more useful than abstract descriptions. Also, be clear about how these analyses will enable you to answer your research questions; you may want to include a version of your questions and methods matrix to illustrate this.

Issues of ethics can be dealt with as part of Methods, but if there are significant ethical questions that could be raised about your study, it may be better to have a separate Ethics section, as Martha Regan-Smith does.

6. Validity

The issue of validity is often dealt with under Methods, but I recommend a separate section for this, for two reasons. The first is clarity—you can explain in one place how you will use different methods to address a single validity threat (a strategy discussed above, known as triangulation), or how a particular validity issue will be dealt with through sampling, data collection, and analysis decisions. The second reason is strategic: devoting a separate section to validity emphasizes that you're taking validity seriously. For this and other issues in a proposal, it is often more important that your reviewers realize that you are *aware* of a particular problem and are thinking about how to deal with it than that you have an airtight plan for solving the problem.

A crucial issue in addressing validity is demonstrating that you will allow for the examination of competing explanations and discrepant data—that your research is not simply a self-fulfilling prophecy. Locke et al. (1993, pp. 92-95) provide a cogent discussion of "the scientific state of mind" and the importance of developing alternative explanations and testing conclusions. In my view, this issue is just as important for qualitative proposals as for quantitative ones.

7. Preliminary Results

If you have already begun your study, this is where you can discuss what you have learned so far about the practicality of your methods or tentative answers to your research questions. This discussion is often valuable in justifying the feasibility of your study and clarifying your methods, particularly your data analysis strategies; see Regan-Smith's proposal for an example of this.

8. Implications (or Conclusions)

This is where you pull together what you've said in the previous sections, remind your readers of the purposes of the study and what it will contribute, and discuss its potential relevance and implications for the broader field(s) that it is situated in. This section should answer any "so what?" questions that might arise in reading the proposal. It is normally fairly short, a page or two at most.

9. References

This section should normally be limited to the references actually cited; unless you are explicitly directed otherwise, it should *not* be a bibliography of relevant literature.

10. Appendices

This may include any of the following:

A timetable for the research

Letters of introduction or permission

Questionnaires, interview guides, or other instruments

A table of interviewees

A schedule of observations

Descriptions of analysis tools

A matrix of relationships between questions, methods, data, and analysis strategies

Examples of observation notes or interview transcripts from pilot studies or completed parts of the study

The appendices can also contain detailed explanations of things (e.g., a particular data collection or analysis technique or background information about your informants or setting) that would require too much space to include in the body of the proposal.

The structure that I present here was originally developed for proposals of about 5,000 words (roughly 20 double-spaced pages). Different departments and funding sources have differing length requirements, some shorter and some longer than this. However, even if your submitted proposal needs to be shorter than this, I would still advise you to write an initial draft of at least 20 pages, because this is a good test of how well you have worked out your design. One student, whose 10-page proposal was approved by his committee, later said,

> I think it would have been better if I had done a more complete proposal. Even though I wasn't sure what form my research was going to take, I still should have spent more time planning. Then I would have had a greater feeling of confidence that I knew where I was going. (Peters, 1992, p. 201)

Once you are confident of your design and how to present this, you can edit this draft down to the required length.

I want to emphasize that your research design can't be mechanically converted into a proposal. Your proposal is a document to *communicate* your design to someone else, and requires careful thinking, separate from the task of designing the research itself, about how best to accomplish this communication. To do this, you need to take into account the particular audience for whom you are writing. Different universities, review boards, government agencies, and foundations all have their own perspectives and standards, and your design needs to be translated into the language and format required or expected by the people who will be reviewing the proposal. The structure I've presented here is a generic one that will in most cases be a good first approximation to what you need, but it may still require more or less adjustment to meet the expectations of your reviewers.

A useful step in moving from the generic proposal structure presented here to a detailed proposal for your specific study is to prepare an outline of the *argument* of your proposal: to develop the actual sequence of points that you need to make to explain and justify your study (see Exercise 7.1). The idea is for you to work specifically on the logic of the proposal, free from the constraints of style and grammatical structure. (For more on how to do this, see Becker, 1986, Chapter 3.) As with concept maps, you can use this exercise in either of two directions—working to develop the logic from scratch and then converting this into a proposal, or taking a draft of your proposal, analyzing this to abstract the argument, and using this argument to revise the proposal.

Example 7.1 provides an outline of the argument of Martha Regan-Smith's proposal, which is presented in full in Appendix A. I have developed this outline from the proposal itself, so it's not a good example of the tentativeness that your own outline will probably exhibit at this point, but

EXAMPLE 7.1
The Argument of a Dissertation Proposal

Argument for a study of how basic science teachers help medical students learn:

1. We need to better understand how basic science teachers in medical school help students learn.
    a. There has been an explosion in the amount of information that needs to be transmitted, with no increase in the time available to teach this.
    b. Medical students' performance on the basic science parts of licensing exams has declined.
    c. These facts have led to student disillusionment and cynicism, and to faculty concern.
2. We know little about how basic science teachers help students learn.
    a. Studies of science teachers in other settings don't necessarily apply to medical schools.
    b. Most research on basic science teaching has been quantitative and doesn't elucidate *how* such teaching helps students learn.
    c. No one has asked medical students what teachers do that helps them to learn.
    d. The research I've already done indicates that students *can* identify what teachers do that helps them learn.
    e. Thus, a qualitative study of basic science teaching, focusing on student perspectives, can make an important contribution.
3. For these reasons, I propose to study four exemplary basic science teachers to understand:
    a. What they do that helps students to learn
    b. How and why this is effective
    c. What motivates these teachers
    d. The relationship between the students' and teachers' perspectives
4. The setting and teachers selected are appropriate for this study.
    a. The medical school to be studied is typical, and my relationship with the school, teachers, and students will facilitate the study.
    b. The teachers selected are appropriate and diverse, and adding additional teachers would not contribute anything significant.
5. The methods I plan to use (participant observation and videotaping of lectures, student and teacher interviews, and documents) will provide the data I need to answer the research questions.
    a. Videotaping provides rich data on what happens in classes and will be used to elicit reflection from the teachers.
    b. Interviews will be open-ended and will incorporate questions based on the observations.

c. The selection of students is guided by theoretical sampling, rather than statistical representativeness, in order to best understand how the teacher helps students.

6. Analysis will generate answers to these questions.

   a. My analysis will be ongoing and inductive in order to identify emergent themes, patterns, and questions.

   b. I will use coding and matrices for comparison across interviews and interview summaries to retain the context of the data.

7. The findings will be validated by:

   a. Triangulating methods

   b. Checks for alternative explanations and negative evidence

   c. Discussion of findings with teachers, students, and colleagues

   d. Comparison of findings with existing theory

   e. These methods, and others described earlier, will enable me to deal with the major validity threats to my conclusions: bias in the selection of teachers and students, and self-report bias for both.

8. The study poses no serious ethical problems.

   a. Teachers and students will be anonymous.

   b. I have taken measures to minimize the possible effect of my own authority.

9. Preliminary results support the practicability and value of the study.

my main purpose is to illustrate what an outline of an argument should look like. Some of the points in this outline are implicit in the proposal, rather than explicit; the extent to which parts of your argument need to be explicitly stated in your proposal depends on what you can assume that your reviewers will easily infer or take for granted. Similarly, the outline itself is only a sketch of what would be necessary to completely justify the study; even in a full proposal, you will not be able to address every possible question about your research, and you will have to focus on those issues that you think are most salient for your audience.

As with my generic model for a proposal structure, I caution you not to use this outline as a *template* for your own argument. Every study needs a different argument in order to adequately justify the research, and in developing this argument you will need to work primarily from your own thinking about your study, not borrow someone else's. In particular, as I discuss in more detail in my comments on Martha Regan-Smith's (1992) proposal, this study is investigating a topic on which little prior work has been done; your argument (and proposal) will almost certainly need to say more about existing theory and research.

Wolcott (1990) provides a useful metaphor to keep in mind as you develop your proposal: "Some of the best advice I've ever seen for writers happened to be included with the directions I found for assembling a new wheelbarrow: *Make sure all parts are properly in place before tightening*" (p. 47). Like a wheelbarrow, your proposal not only needs to have all the required parts, it has to *work*—to be put together so that it functions smoothly and conveys to others your research design and the justification for this. This requires attention to the connections between the different parts of the proposal and to how well the proposal as a written document can be understood by your intended audience. As described above, these are two aspects of what I call coherence. A coherent proposal depends on a coherent design, but it also needs its own coherence, to flow clearly from beginning to end without gaps, obscurities, confusing transitions, or red herrings. As I've emphasized, there isn't One Right Way to do this; I've tried to give you the tools that will enable you to put together *a* way that works for you and your research.

EXERCISE 7.1
Developing an Argument for Your Proposal

The purpose of the exercise is for you to outline the argument of your proposal, not its detailed content or structure. You want to present the main substantive points that you need to make about your study, and to organize these so there is a clear logic that leads to a justification for the study. These arguments do not have to be developed in the full form that they will have in the proposal itself, but they should provide the essence of the latter and should form a coherent sequence.

If you are in the beginning stages of planning your proposal, the outline can be very hypothetical and tentative; the purpose of the exercise is for you to start working on developing your argument, not for you to commit yourself to anything. At this point, it's not important whether you have any evidence or citations to back up your claims; after you have developed an outline of your argument, you can then assess where the holes are in your evidence, and what you need to do to fill them. This exercise is, in Marydee Spillett's phrase, a "come as you are" party; construct the best argument you can with your present knowledge.

NOTES

1. This doesn't mean that you should *conceal* your political views; these are an appropriate part of the discussion of your purposes and may be a possible validity threat

that you want to address. However, the discussion should focus on how these views inform your design, rather than being political polemic or irrelevant self-display.

2. Locke et al. (1993, pp. 66-80) provide an excellent discussion of the purposes and construction of a literature review. However, the literature review in their example qualitative proposal is longer than necessary and less coherent than you want yours to be.

3. The term "methodology" is often used for this section of a proposal. Despite its prevalence, this is an inaccurate and pretentious usage, a good example of what Becker (1986) calls classy writing. Methodology is the theory or analysis of methods, not what you actually do in a particular study.

4. For some suggestions on how to justify a qualitative study to a potentially ignorant or hostile audience, see Maxwell (1993).

5. Robson (1993, pp. 465-469) and Locke et al. (1993, pp. 145-182) discuss the specific requirements of funding proposals.

Appendix A:
An Example of a
Qualitative Proposal

No single proposal can adequately represent the diversity of qualitative research designs and ways of communicating these. If space permitted, I would include two or three proposals here, to emphasize that there is no one right way to structure either a qualitative study or a proposal. Because I can present only one, I've chosen Martha Regan-Smith's proposal for her dissertation, a study of exemplary medical school teachers. Not only does it give a clear, straightforward explanation and justification for the proposed study, but it raises many of the key issues that most qualitative proposals will have to address. In my commentary, I try to identify and clarify the connections between these issues and my model of research design, and to present alternative ways of handling these issues. The proposal appears here just as Regan-Smith submitted it, with only a few additions (marked by brackets) or corrections of typos or punctuation for greater clarity; the appendices and references have been omitted.

The most serious danger in presenting an exemplary proposal such as this is that you might use it as a *template* for your own proposal, borrowing its structure and language and simply "filling in the blanks" with your own study. This is a sure recipe for disaster. Your proposal needs to fit the study that you are proposing, and an argument that works well for one study may totally fail to justify a different study. Construct your proposal around your *own* design, not someone else's.

HOW BASIC SCIENCE TEACHERS
HELP MEDICAL STUDENTS LEARN:
THE STUDENTS' PERSPECTIVE

Dissertation Proposal

Martha G. Regan-Smith

March 6, 1991

Harvard Graduate School of Education

Abstract

Medical school consists of 2 years of basic science and 2 years of clinical training. The sciences taught in the first 2 years include Anatomy, Biochemistry, Physiology, Pathology, Microbiology, and Pharmacology. As a result of the biomedical information expansion which has occurred in the last 80 years with no increase in the time available to teach this information, the teaching of basic science has become content heavy. In addition, the teaching has become increasingly rapid paced as most schools over the past 20 years have decreased the number of hours spent in laboratories and demonstrations while increasing reliance on lecturing as the way to teach. Medical student performance on the basic science examinations used for licensure has decreased, and, as a result, medical school faculty feel medical student learning of basic science is less than desired.

As a member of medical school faculties for 18 years, I want to improve medical student learning of basic science by improving the teaching of basic science in medical school. No qualitative studies of basic science teaching in medical school exist. What works for student learning and how it works is not known. In order to understand how teachers can help medical students learn basic science, I propose to do a qualitative study of four exceptional basic science teachers to answer the following research questions: How do these basic science teachers help medical students learn? What do these teachers do to help students learn? How and why do these techniques help students learn? What motivates the teachers to do what they do? Is what students feel teachers do to help them learn what teachers intend? How do student understandings of what helps them learn differ from teacher understandings?

Each of the four teachers studied teaches a different basic science at a typical private medical school in the northeastern United States. The school has a traditional curriculum in which the 2 years of basic science are taught predominantly using the lecture format. Each teacher is a winner of the student-selected Best Teacher Award, and each teacher uses the lecture format for his teaching.

Participant observation of the teachers' lectures and teacher and student interviews are the primary data sources. Classes, in addition, are audiotaped for transcription and videotaped. Videotapes are analyzed as well as used as prompts for dialogue when shown to teachers or students. Interviews are tape-recorded, transcribed, and coded. Analytic memos are written and coded for each class observation and interview. Matrices are constructed to identify themes and to check evolving concepts. Both teacher and student collaboration is obtained by getting their opinions of my analysis and conclusions. Each teacher's teaching is analyzed separately followed by comparative analysis of all four teachers' teaching. Generated theory will be compared to existing theory, which is primarily based in other educational settings or on personal experience. The goal is to identify teaching techniques and behaviors that help students learn and to gain understanding of how and why these techniques help students learn. This knowledge about practice in context can be taught to teachers in faculty development workshops designed to teach teachers how to improve their teaching. By teaching teachers how to better help students learn, it is hoped that improved student learning will result.

This abstract is a concise summary, not just of the components of the research design, but of the connections between these—the *argument* of the proposal. Standards and requirements for abstracts vary, but conveying the argument of your proposal should be a primary goal.

Table of Contents

Methods of Data Collection
  Videotaping
  Student Interviews
  Teacher Interviews
Methods of Analysis
  Single-Case Analysis
  Cross-Case Analysis
Validity Issues
Ethical Issues
Preliminary Findings
Appendices

Introduction

Since the Flexner Report in 1910, the 4-year medical school curriculum has comprised 2 years of teaching the sciences basic to
medicine followed by 2 years of training in the clinical disciplines.
The basic sciences include Anatomy, Microbiology, Biochemistry,
Pharmacology, Pathology, and Physiology, and the clinical disciplines
include Surgery, Medicine, Pediatrics, Psychiatry, and Obstetrics/
Gynecology. Because of the information explosion in biomedical
science during the past 80 years, the basic science curriculum has
become "overstuffed" (Eichna, 1980). Usually three to four sciences
are taught simultaneously, using predominantly the lecture format. As
a result, students are in class 25-33 hours per week throughout the first
2 years of medical school. This, combined with the student perception
of ineffective teaching (Awbrey, 1985; Eichna, 1980; Jonas, 1978;
Konner, 1987), has led to student disillusionment with science (Eichna,
1980) and student cynicism about the educational process (Petersdorf,
1987). In addition, the national failure rate on the basic science portion
of the National Board of Medical Examiners examinations has risen
over the past 6 years (NBME letter to Deans, Appendix A) without a
demonstrable decrease in student undergraduate grade point averages
or admission examination scores.

In an effort to improve the teaching of basic science in medical
school, I want to study what teachers of basic science actually do to
help medical students learn. I propose to conduct a qualitative study
of four exceptional basic science teachers' teaching, from the students'
perspective, to answer the question, "How do these teachers help
medical students learn?" The goal is to identify teaching techniques

and behaviors that help students learn, which can then be taught to teachers in faculty development workshops designed to teach teachers how to improve their teaching and hence better assist student learning.

In this Introduction, Martha sets the stage for what follows by presenting the practical problem that motivates the study and the historical context of this problem and briefly stating the nature of the proposed study. Details of the context, research questions, and methods are left for later. Different studies will require different amounts of information in order to adequately accomplish this task of orienting the reader to the study itself and to what will follow in the proposal.

Context

To increase medical student enthusiasm for and learning of basic science, several scholars have called for critical examination of the teaching of basic sciences (Beaty, 1990; Bishop, 1984; Neame, 1984). A small number of schools, such as McMaster and Harvard, have been able to replace lectures with small-group tutorials during which students participate in problem-based learning by independently solving paper patient cases (Neufeld & Barrows, 1974; Schmidt, 1983). Most medical schools, however, because of financial and faculty constraints, must continue to rely on lectures as a major method of teaching basic sciences. Therefore investigation of how the lecture method can be effective in assisting student learning is worthwhile.

This paragraph justifies studying the lecture method of teaching basic science. It works well here but could just as easily have been part of the Introduction.

Existing Literature on Basic
Science Teaching in Medical School

Studies of science teaching in secondary or undergraduate schools do not necessarily apply to the medical school setting. The teaching of science through the use of lectures in medical school is unlike the teaching of science in any other educational setting. The rapid pace of medical school and the vast quantity of material needed to be learned by students with varying science backgrounds make the teaching of science and the learning by the students unique. Effective teaching through the use of lectures in nonmedical school educational settings has been well-described and studied (Eble, 1976; Hyman, 1974; Katona, 1940; McKeachie, 1969), but whether the teaching techniques recommended are appropriate in the medical school setting or whether other techniques are helpful is unknown. Qualitative study asking students what works for their learning is needed. The medical education and health professions education literature on lecturing is limited. Some prescriptive works on how to give effective lectures (Bughman, 1973; Miller, 1962) are based on implicit theory derived from personal experience as students and as faculty (Cook, 1989). Others have been written by educators working in the medical school arena (Jason, 1982), but these are based on educational theory derived from educational settings other than medical school. Schwenk and Whitman (1987) prescribe effective lecturing techniques related to existing educational theory and relate these techniques to communication theory and negotiation theory inherent in effective doctor/patient relationships.

Quantitative studies of lecturing in medical school, usually utilizing student ratings of lecturing techniques, depend on the researchers' prior understanding and assumptions about what helps students learn. Because no qualitative studies of medical student learning of basic science exist, this understanding is based on theory derived from study of or experience with nonmedical school settings. The few quantitative studies in the literature looking at basic science teaching in medical school (Mendez, 1984; Naftulin, 1973; Russell, 1984; Ware, 1975) are limited in scope and contribute little to the research question, "How do basic science teachers help medical students learn?"

Naftulin (1973), looking at teaching delivered in a "seductive charismatic manner," showed that students could give high ratings of such teaching; however, the audience's perception of learning was not included in the study. In response, Ware (1975) concluded that "seductive, charismatic lecturers" assist student learning by showing that students attending lectures with high seduction (characterized by enthusiasm, humor, friendliness, expressiveness, charisma, personality) and low content have similar examination scores as students attending low seduction, high content lectures. How these teacher characteristics contribute to student learning of content was not addressed. Mendez (1984) surveyed year I and II medical students for the factors contributing to lecture attendance and found that students attend lectures that they perceive to have clearly defined objectives and that cover material tested on the final examination. How the objectives help student learning and which lecture techniques help learning were not investigated. Russell (1984) looked at medical student retention of basic material immediately after and 15 days following lectures with varying amounts of content and found that increasing information density of lectures reduced retention of the basic information. The reasons for this effect were not a part of the study.

Slotnick (1975) and Irby (1976), using quantitative methods, demonstrated that teaching criteria presumed by the researchers to be important for student learning were in fact important to students for their learning. Slotnick (1975) showed that faculty-student rapport, student work required outside of class, pace of class, overall workload, understandability of lecture material, lecturing activities (e.g., summary of material, concise explanation, organization of material in a logical way), student ability to organize material, and professor knowledge of students' knowledge level are interrelated rather than univariate factors in effective teaching. How these factors affect student learning and why was not a part of the study. Irby (1976) showed that teachers could improve their teaching when given immediate feedback about student ratings of their teaching. The rating variables were derived from education literature, and whether the list of teaching techniques rated by the students included all the techniques helpful for student learning could not be determined from the study.

No one has asked medical students what teachers do to help them learn. Existing research has asked students to rate particular teaching techniques or to state whether a technique works or not. These studies depend on the researchers' understanding of what works for student learning. What works to help students learn science in other educational settings may not work in medical school. Quite possibly basic science teachers in medical school have happened upon or developed teaching techniques that are unique to medical school or are unintentionally assisting learning in ways they do not appreciate. Qualitative study is needed to generate a theory of effective nonclinical teaching in medical school.

This section of the proposal argues that we know very little about how basic science teachers in medical school help their students to learn. This point is important in justifying a qualitative study of this phenomenon. As a result, however, the proposal says little about what will be the focus of the Context sections of most proposals: existing theory about, and research on, the phenomenon studied. Martha Regan-Smith briefly reviews several theories about what constitutes effective teaching in medical school lectures, but her main point is that these studies address neither *how* such teaching methods work nor the students' perspective. If your study is of a topic for which there exists a substantial literature of theory and research, your Context section will need to address this literature, as well as your own experience (which Regan-Smith discusses in the next section) and pilot research (which she deals with both in the next section and later, under Preliminary Findings).

Personal Interest

I am a physician, an internist, and rheumatologist. I was a chemistry major in college, and, prior to this study, I had not participated in a science class since I was a medical student 21 years ago. I have taught how to diagnose adult disease in clinical medicine for 18 years. Approximately 6 years ago I realized I was also trying to teach both critical thinking skills and the communication skills needed to enable others to understand the reasoning behind a diagnosis. I also realized that I did not know much about critical thinking or communication, let alone how to effectively teach these skills. In 1987 I entered the [Harvard Graduate School of Education] master's program to learn about these skills and how they can be taught. I felt these skills should be a part of a physician's education, and I quickly learned that effective learning of these skills necessitated teaching of these skills throughout medical school, not just in clinical medicine courses.

In 1988, for a course on perspectives of teaching, I was required to study a teacher, classroom, or school. I chose to study a teacher. As the Assistant Dean for Clinical Education, whose responsibility is to oversee all clinical teaching, I anticipated I could more easily gain entry into a teacher's classroom if I chose to study a basic science teacher rather than a clinical teacher. In addition, I chose to study a winner of the student-awarded Best Teacher Award. I reasoned that I could learn more about teaching from a winner of such an accolade than a nonwinner, and that a winner would be more likely (i.e., have more confidence) to allow my presence in his classroom than a nonwinner.

I expected the teacher to be skillful; however, I was awed by the extent of his skill as a teacher. Equally surprising was how articulate the students were at describing how he helped them learn. Although I appreciated how he helped me learn in the classroom, I needed student input to appreciate all the aspects of what he did and why it worked for them. Curiosity about how other teachers help medical students learn basic science, and my desire to improve medical education, led to my application in 1988 to the doctoral program, with plans to pursue study of how basic science teachers help students learn. By finding out, from the students' perspective, what works to help students learn, I want to discover how teachers can help their students learn and why. Two more teachers have been studied as part of methods courses: the most recent was written up as my qualifying paper entitled, "Relevance in Teaching." Each teacher has exemplified all the teaching characteristics that I identified as helping students learn; however, each teacher has best exemplified a different teaching characteristic. The information gleaned from these teacher studies can be used in faculty development workshops designed to teach teachers how to better help their students learn.

In this section, Regan-Smith describes how the study originated, presenting her personal purposes and how these connect to the practical and theoretical purposes described in the Introduction. She also describes her own background as the "research instrument" of the study. In doing all this, she also begins to build her justification for the selection of exemplary teachers as the focus of the study, and for using students as a major source of data.

Proposed Research

Research Goals

I want to learn what teachers do to help students learn. The teaching techniques gleaned from teachers in practice, which I identify as helping students learn, will be useful for other teachers to improve their teaching. Quantitative researchers define the problems of practice in their own terms, not the terms of the practitioners, and tend to generate knowledge that is not useful to the practitioner (Bolster, 1983). Quantitative research often does not cause change in practice, whereas qualitative research, which strives to understand the meaning of action to the participants, can offer improvement of arguments for practice and hence can have greater effect on practice (Fenstermacher, 1986). Knowledge generated by quantitative educational research is often not useful to practitioners, who are swayed more by practical arguments, experience, and faith (Buchmann, 1984). To improve practice, educational research needs to emphasize the context within which the activities studied occur and the meanings of activities studied for the participants. Qualitative research methods meet these needs (Abrahamson, 1984).

The unique teaching/learning situation in the first 2 years of medical school merits a qualitative research design that (a) takes into account the contextual elements that make medical education different from other science education settings and (b) allows for inductive hypothesis generation. What works for basic science lectures is unknown. What helps medical students learn may well be different than what works for students of science in other settings. There is a need for students to define and explain what works. Understanding how particular methods work will require understanding of the context. Using qualitative research methods to study teachers and their students in basic science lecture-format classrooms, I intend to learn from the students and their teachers how basic science teachers help students learn.

For my dissertation, I propose to study four basic science teachers. Recognizing that students can be valid, reliable, and useful evaluators of teaching (Costin, 1971; Irby, 1977; Palchik, 1988; Rippey, 1975), I decided to continue to study student-selected Best Teacher Award winners. I will analyze each teacher's teaching individually and then comparatively analyze the data collected from all four teacher studies. The theory generated about basic science teaching will be compared to existing effective teaching theory generated from other educational settings.

In this section, Regan-Smith reviews the main question and purposes of the study and uses these to justify a qualitative study. In the process, she brings in two additional pieces of the conceptual context that relate particularly to methods: the relatively greater impact of qualitative research on practice and the validity of student ratings of teaching. This discussion could just as easily have been included in the Context section.

Research Questions

The research questions to be answered are: How do these basic science teachers help their students learn? What do these teachers do to help students learn? How and why do these techniques help students learn? What motivates teachers to do what they do? Is what students feel teachers do to help them learn what teachers intend? How do student understandings of what helps them learn differ from teacher understandings?

In this section, Regan-Smith expands on the single main question she stated in the Introduction, specifying the range of questions and subquestions that she will address. In many proposals, more explanation or justification of the questions would be desirable, but because of the clear rationale that Regan-Smith provides for these questions in previous sections, it seems unnecessary here. For clarity, it is often better to number your research questions, and to indicate which of these are subquestions of particular main questions.

Research Site

I chose to study teachers at a private northeastern medical school where I have been on the faculty for 10 years (I was a winner of the Best Teacher Award for clinical teaching in 1987), and I have been the Assistant Dean for Clinical Education for 4 years. The school is a typical private medical school of slightly less than average student body size. It has a traditional curriculum with 2 years of basic science followed by 2 years of clinical experience.

The students are 50% to 65% males and 35% to 50% females and come from over 50 different public and private schools throughout the United States. Passage of the National Board of Medical Examiners examinations is not required for promotion or graduation; however, most students take the examinations to obtain licensure to practice. The school's matriculating students' admission grade point averages and admission examination scores are near or slightly above the national mean. During the past 5 years, the school's students' failure rate on the basic science portion of the National Board of Medical Examiners examinations has been at or near the national failure rate and has risen as the national failure rate has. The only differentiating features of this school from other U.S. medical schools are its rural location and its close, friendly faculty/student rapport.

I have professional relationships of considerable mutual respect with the teachers I have chosen to study. All have worked with me as colleagues on Dean's Advisory, Curriculum, and/or Student Performance Committees. We see each other as education advocates in an environment that does not reward education program development or teaching achievement. The four teachers chosen from the Best Teacher list to be studied each teach at least 20 hours of different basic science discipline courses (Appendix B) and primarily use the lecture format. The basic science teacher winners that will not be studied either teach the same discipline as another studied teacher or teach using a non-lecture method (see Appendix B).

Three teacher observations and interviews have been completed. The teacher remaining to be studied is to be included because he has passion for his subject, which is a recognized dimension of effective teaching (Eble, 1976). Students participating in my previous studies of medical school basic science teaching have recommended study of this professor, who teaches Pathology, because they perceive him as best exemplifying love of subject, which they feel is very important for their learning.

In this section, Regan-Smith accomplishes two purposes. First, she describes the setting of her proposed study (supporting the generalizability of her results) and the kind of study she plans to do and further justifies her choice of teachers. Second, she explains some aspects of her research relationship with the teachers she will be studying. The proposal would have been stronger if she had said more about this and about her relationship with the students.

Methods of Data Collection

Qualitative research methods were selected for this study both because I did not know a priori what I would find and because I wanted to generate data rich in detail and embedded in context. Classroom participant observation, student interviews, and teacher interviews are the primary sources [methods] of data collection. In addition, course outlines, syllabi, quizzes, examinations and examination results, paper cases, slides, and other handouts are collected as data. Student evaluations of the course and of the teacher's teaching are also used if available.

For all case studies I attend all possible scheduled lectures given by the teacher throughout a 4-month course. This will be no less than two thirds of the teacher's teaching. Two to four lectures are audiotaped to record exactly what was said by the teacher and students in the classroom and later transcribed. As discussed below, I videotape teachers teaching and interview both students and teachers. I take fieldnotes while in class, unless I am videotaping, and write analytic memos and contact summaries (Miles & Huberman, 1984) following each class as well as each interview.

These two paragraphs provide an overview of the Methods section as a whole, and explain the sampling strategy for her observations. The sampling of students is dealt with later, under Student Interviews.

Videotaping

Videotaping, which I first used with the third teacher I observed, produces a rich source of data about what is going on in the classroom. It allows me to see things I could not see otherwise. I will have the opportunity to review classroom action and observe and isolate individual parts of what is going on. Several of the videotapes will also be used to facilitate the teacher discussing his own teaching in depth. By showing the teacher the tapes of his teaching, I can ask about individual components of his teaching in context. In addition, the tapes will be used to stimulate student dialogue. They will be shown to students to facilitate their explaining the effect of what the teacher does in the classroom to help their learning. Since videotaping was not used to study all four teachers, a comparative analysis cannot be done including all teachers.

Note that videotaping serves two different purposes in this study: ensuring the descriptive validity of her observations, and stimulating recall and reflection as a component of some of the interviews with teachers and students. Videotaping only two of the four teachers would be a serious flaw if the primary purpose of this study were to compare the teachers, but it is not; the primary goal is to obtain an in-depth understanding of each of the four teachers, and it would be pointless to forgo the advantages of videotaping the last two teachers simply to maintain a superficial consistency of method. In a proposal that will be reviewed by readers not familiar with qualitative research, such a decision might need more explicit justification.

Student Interviews

The student interviews begin with an open-ended question such as "What stands out for you?" or "What did you notice?" Subsequent questions are conversational in an attempt to get the interviewee to discuss further something he/she mentioned in an answer. For the first several interviews, the only other preconceived question is "What does the teacher do that helps you learn?" As I observe more classes, questions arise for which I need answers in order to confirm my observation conclusions and to understand what is going on in the classroom, and these are added. Eventually a set of questions (Appendix C) emerge from the evolving data; I ask these questions of all remaining interviewees in addition to the two original set questions.

Out of a class of 84 students, 10 to 20 formal student interviews, lasting 20-45 minutes each, are conducted for each teacher study. As many of the student interviews as time will allow are done after the final examination to minimize student fear that what they say will affect their grade. The interviews occur in my office and are audiotaped and later transcribed. Each interview is preceded by my stating that I am studying what teachers do in the classroom to help students learn, and all interviews are kept anonymous. Analytic memos and contact summary sheets discussing setting, student attitude and demeanor, and content are written for each interview.

The students I interview are selected to contribute student opinion and characteristics that seem important to the context of the study. In the three concluded studies and planned for the fourth study, I seek samples of the student population guided by my emerging theory using theoretical sampling (Strauss, 1987). I do not attempt to get an empirically "representative" sample. As I learn about and make sense of the events in the classroom and its meaning to the participants, I look for negative data as well as positive data for my emerging theory. I determine how many interviews I will do by doing interviews until I find that I am discovering nothing new. I purposely interview students known to be outspoken and critical to be sure I hear negative comments, as well as students known to be outsiders (loners—not a member of one of the cliques in the class) to be sure to get different opinions rather than just "the party line." By asking interviewees to tell me who in the class has opinions about the class and the teacher different from their own, I find out which students are likely to provide contrasting perspectives. In addition, I try to interview students who do not regularly attend class in an effort to understand what informs their decisions to attend or not to attend class.

In this section, Regan-Smith presents and justifies both her sampling strategy for the student interviews and how she will conduct them. Again, the lack of uniformity of interview questions for all students would be a flaw if the purpose of the study were to compare student responses, but it is not. The number of student interviews could have received more explicit justification, but most readers would feel that this is a more than adequate number. Further justification for her sampling decisions are provided in her discussion of validity, and these decisions are supported by her preliminary results.

Teacher Interviews

For all four studies, the teacher is interviewed formally three to six times, and all interviews are audiotaped and transcribed. The interviews occur throughout the course as well as after the course if appropriate. In general, the interview questions are about issues about which I become curious as an observer in class or as the result of student input. I pursue issues raised by the teacher and ask preconceived questions only if the teacher does not spontaneously address an issue of interest to me.

Formal teacher interviews last at least 30-55 minutes. For two of the teachers, I will use a class videotape as "text for dialogue" about the teacher's teaching for at least one interview. This yields more specific information about the teacher's play-by-play reasoning and strategy than interviews without videotapes, which tend to yield more abstract general teaching strategies and attitudes. Data gathered is analyzed along with the class observations in daily analytic memos and contact sheet summaries.

Because Regan-Smith had already collected much of her data when she wrote this proposal, she has a dilemma with what tense to use. Her decision to use mostly present tense seems to be the best choice; this could be misleading, but she has clearly explained earlier that she has already completed data collection for three of the four teachers. For dissertation proposals, I advise you to be completely candid about how much of your data you have already collected, unless you receive knowledgeable advice to the contrary. For funding proposals, this may be unwise; seek specific advice from those familiar with the particular funding source.

Methods of Analysis

Single Case-Study Analysis

Analysis of collected data is ongoing. Analysis of transcribed interviews and classes is coded during data collection as soon as transcriptions are available. Codes are inductively generated using the "grounded" approach of Glaser (1965) and emerge from the participants' descriptions of the teacher's teaching. In addition, coding is done using codes from a "start list" (Miles & Huberman, 1984) generated from previous studies. All interviews and classroom transcripts are reread specifically for codes that emerge from later interviews. As patterns or themes are identified, dimensionalization (Strauss & Corbin, 1990) is carried out accompanied by recoding for the developed dimensions or properties of a given theme. Matrices are constructed from the data and are used to identify patterns, comparisons, trends, and paradoxes. Further questions and possible routes of inquiry are devised to answer the questions that emerge from matrices. Periodic review of all the collected data, as well as all the analytic memos, followed by summary construction and formulation of yet to be answered questions is done every 2 or 3 weeks throughout the study. In addition, I meet weekly with an education colleague, knowledgeable about qualitative research and the research site, to summarize the status of the research and to discuss emerging themes, concepts, and explanations.

In the final phase of data analysis, each interview is reread with the objective of writing individual short interview summaries. These summaries allow me to see threads that run through interviews and thereby maintain the context for the quotes that are lifted out of the interviews and used as examples in writing up the research. Using Microsoft Word (Apple, 1988), I then cut and paste quotes from all the interviews, creating new separate documents for each code that had emerged from analysis of the interviews. This compilation of quotes for each code is used to appreciate trends, contrasts, and similarities. Matrices are constructed to check the validity of themes that emerge. Finally, the data are reviewed to pair up student perspectives with teacher perspectives of the same phenomenon to compare and contrast perspectives, as well as to look at whether what the teacher intends is, in fact, what the students perceive as happening.

Validation of data is achieved by triangulation (Denzin, 1970) of methods by comparing student perspectives, teacher perspectives, and participant observer perspectives of events in the classroom. Theoretical validation is achieved by regular presentation and discussion of emerging conclusions with medical school colleagues familiar with the setting, students, and teachers. Further validation is achieved by discussing my analyses and conclusions with the teacher and with students.

Cross-Case Analysis

Once I develop an understanding about how the fourth teacher helps his students learn, I will begin cross-case analysis. The first step will be construction of a conceptual framework (Miles & Huberman,

1984) containing the dominant themes of how these four teachers help students learn. Each theme will be dimensionalized (Strauss & Corbin, 1990) or broken into factors and graphically displayed, illustrating the relationships between them.

Patterns and themes will be sought by construction of cross-case displays and matrices. Plausible explanations and metaphors will emerge as the variables are related, split, and factored (Miles & Huberman, 1984). The goal will be to build a logical chain of evidence (Scriven, 1974) and to construct a theoretically and conceptually coherent theory by checking for rival explanations and looking for negative evidence. In order to check for theory validation, informants will be asked for feedback on generated theory after data collection is completed.

Regan-Smith's description of her analysis strategies is detailed and comprehensive but rather abstract and boilerplate, and it doesn't give a good sense of the actual methods and categories she'll use. This weakness is compensated for by her discussion of Preliminary Findings, below, which provides detailed, concrete examples of the *content* of her analysis. The discussion of evidence, rival explanations, and feedback also paves the way for the next section, on validity.

Validity Issues

1. *Teacher selection*: After the fourth teacher study, I will have studied the award winners from four different discipline courses who use the lecture method (Appendix B). I will stop at four teachers, unless another important teaching characteristic is identified that I have not already found. Because the study school has no features that make it different from other U.S. medical schools with a traditional curriculum of 2 years of basic science and 2 years of clinical experience, I find no reason to study teachers elsewhere. Most teachers of basic science in most schools are male, so I found no validity threat to my study by the teachers being male.

This is really an argument for the *generalizability* of her results, not their validity.

2. *Student selection:* Did I interview enough students? Did I bias the data by who I interviewed? I intentionally try to interview students who have different perspectives and opinions of the teacher's teach-

ing. I interview students who are: (a) known to be outspokenly critical of teaching, (b) from all quartiles of the class, (c) from a variety of career choices, (d) whom I know and whom I barely know, (e) who are referred to me by classmates as feeling different about the class and teacher, (f) who participate in the typical camaraderie of the class and who do not, and (g) who attend most every class and who attend only a few. In essence, I try to seek out students who do not feel the teacher helps them learn as well as those who do. Thereby I try to get both negative and positive student input. I stop interviewing when I begin to hear the same things repeated and no new information.

This paragraph deals with some plausible threats to the validity of her results. The sampling strategy described here is an example of purposeful sampling; the decision on when to stop interviewing is based on what Strauss (1987) calls *theoretical saturation.*

3. *How do I know what students say is true and not just what I want to hear* (i.e., that the teacher helped them learn when he did not)? To make students comfortable being honest with me, I assure the students anonymity and interview them in a location distant from the classroom. As often as possible, I postpone student interviews until after student grades have been awarded. I also attempt to interview students who are scheduled to finish their third and fourth years at another medical school, thereby eliminating any power I may have as Dean for Clinical Education over them. In the three completed studies, students have not held back from criticizing the teachers nor sharing with me their negative feelings and opinions of the teachers' teaching. I use my presence in the classroom as a learner trying to understand new subjects (e.g., the molecular biology of viruses) to substantiate whether a teacher truly helps students learn. If the teacher helps me learn and the students say he helps them and they pass the course, I believe them. I ask students to give examples of all teaching characteristics they claim help them learn, and then I substantiate student examples by being present in class. Collaboration with students (both those included in the study and those who were not) by discussing my observations and my conclusions also helps increase my confidence in the validity of my work.

This paragraph addresses her relationship with the students, which has ethical as well as validity implications, and argues that her relationship to them as Dean is not a validity threat to her conclusions.

Someone who didn't know Regan-Smith and her reputation among these
students might not find this argument completely convincing, but I'm not
sure what else she could say. The most persuasive point, for me, is that
the students she has interviewed *have* been critical of their teachers.

4. *How do I know what the teacher says he does is true?* I substantiate all teacher claims by participant observation and through student
interviews. Teacher beliefs and stated reasons for behavior are accepted as true unless I encounter discrepant evidence.

Here, Regan-Smith basically relies on triangulation to deal with the
validity threat of self-report bias in the teacher interviews. She could
also have used the argument she made in discussing the student
interviews: that, having already studied three of the teachers, she
knows that the observations and student interviews corroborate the
teachers' reports.

This section as a whole is organized by particular validity threats—
how she might be wrong. In discussing these threats, Martha draws on
information previously presented in the Methods section but reorgan-
izes this information so it's clear how the data obtained through these
methods will help her to deal with these threats.

Ethical Issues

Could my research harm the students or teachers? The teachers risk
my finding out that they are not as good at teaching as their award
would merit. Even though I do not oversee the basic science part of
the curriculum, my administrative colleagues do; and I am a member
of the Curriculum Committee. To minimize this fear of risk, each
teacher is assured that no one other than specified study school
education colleagues with whom I discuss results and conclusions
(and my thesis readers) will know of the results of my research unless
the teacher gives me permission to do otherwise. I cannot eliminate
this risk for the teachers.

No harm from teachers can come to the students who participate
because the students' identities are kept secret. I cannot eliminate the
risk that I, as the Dean who writes the student's letter of recommendation for residency after graduation, will form opinions about them
as a result of my interview. Those students concerned about such a
risk can easily avoid participation. I am aware of no one refusing to
participate when asked, hence I do not think student avoidance of
participation poses a significant validity threat to my research.

This section could be placed either before or after Validity. One point that could have been made explicitly here is that these teachers, as award winners, have less to fear from examination of their teaching than most teachers. Regan-Smith could also have dealt more convincingly with the ethical issue of risk to the students. Ultimately, her argument depends on her own integrity. The point at the end, about validity, belongs in the previous section.

Preliminary Findings

To date, preliminary analysis of the data has enabled me to identify a number of teaching characteristics that help students learn: clarity, relevance, knowledge of students' understanding, teaching to different learning styles, and passion for the subject. Each of the three teachers studied so far has been found to best exemplify different teaching characteristics, even though the characteristics were found in all the other teachers' teaching. In other words, the characteristics identified that help medical students learn basic science are practiced by all the teachers studied but each teacher is a "master" at one or two different characteristics.

The first teacher teaches heart physiology, anatomy, and clinical disease to Year II students as a part of the Scientific Basis of Medicine course. The students felt that his lecture style was "like a conversation" with them; the students felt he understood what they knew and what they did not. In addition, this teacher addressed multiple student learning styles by presenting the course material (e.g., coronary artery disease) in seven different ways (i.e. lecture, reading assignments with clear stated objectives, computer interactive patient cases, student participation in demonstrations, small group discussions, problem solving of paper cases, and student presentations of current articles to small groups).

The second teacher teaches the virology section of the Microbiology course in Year I. The students and the teacher felt that the most important feature of his teaching was clarity. The students perceived him to achieve clarity by (a) limiting the material needed to learn, (b) explicitly defining the material the students need and do not need to know, (c) specifying the meaning of his words, (d) presenting concepts moving from the simple to the complex in a logical progression, (e) including stories about patients, epidemiological problems, or medical history to explain concepts, (f) asking the class questions critical to understanding the concepts, and (g) repetition of key concepts and facts. He checks on his clarity by giving weekly quizzes and spending extra time in class to explain any quiz questions missed by a significant number of students. The quizzes promote clarity for the students because they additionally give the students feedback on what they know and do not know as well as force them to learn the material weekly and keep up with learning the material rather than cramming for the final examination.

The third teacher teaches pharmacology and best exemplifies the use of relevance in teaching. He uses relevance in his classroom teaching by structuring each lecture around either a presentation of a patient case of his own or a patient case volunteered by a student. In addition, each week he provides students with paper case problems to solve individually, thereby letting students simulate practice as physicians. Relevance is also achieved by having students teach students how to solve the case problems. The ensuing class discussion allows students (and the teacher) to learn and discuss student understanding of the pharmacologic principles. The use of the Socratic method by this teacher as cases are discussed in class gives the students opportunity to privately reflect on their own similar experiences with patients. Relevance is also achieved by students privately conversing during class, relating to a neighbor what they are learning in class to cases they have seen, and sharing the experience with the classmate.

Previously studied teachers were not aware of all they did in the classroom to help students learn. Often a teacher is unable to fully appreciate how he helps students learn without my feedback. From the fourth teacher, I expect to learn how a teacher's passion for or love of subject helps students learn. I have heard the fourth teacher speak and he is mesmerizing. His charismatic style of presentation captures the audience's attention and, I suppose, it helps them remember what he says. He may also contribute to their learning by motivating them to learn on their own.

I expect the comparative analysis to reveal that the dimensions of each of the individual teachers' teaching characteristics overlap (e.g., anecdotes used to achieve clarity also achieve relevance). Ongoing analysis of my first three case studies reveals that students feel that student-involved teaching, such as students teaching students, is particularly useful for their learning because it achieves clarity, relevance, and a form of student/teacher conversation, and it addresses student learning styles.

This discussion of preliminary findings serves several purposes. First, it supports Martha's argument that the methods she proposes are workable and will allow her to generate interesting and valid answers to her questions. Second, it fleshes out her rather abstract and general discussion of data analysis, clarifying how she is coding her data and integrating themes within each case, and suggesting issues that the cross-case analysis will focus on.

In summary, by using qualitative research methods to study basic science teachers who primarily use the lecture format to teach, I intend to find how these teachers help medical students learn. The theory generated will be compared to existing theory on effective teaching using lectures in other educational settings. This theory will be used to develop faculty workshops to teach teachers how to teach. The ultimate goal of improved basic science teaching in medical school is to improve medical student enthusiasm for, and learning of, the sciences basic to medicine.

This final paragraph sums up the study by briefly reviewing, in the reverse order from their presentation in the proposal, four components of the design: the methods, the research question, the theoretical context, and the purposes of the study. In doing this, it clearly shows the connections between these components and links the proposed research to the purposes with which the proposal began. However, this is pretty terse for a conclusions section; most proposals will need to say more to summarize the proposal and present the implications of the study.

Appendix B:
Recommended Resources

Glesne, C., & Peshkin, A. (1992). *Becoming qualitative researchers: An introduction.* White Plains, NY: Longman.

Weiss, R. S. (1994). *Learning from strangers: The art and method of qualitative interviewing.* New York: Free Press.

These (along with Becker, 1986) are the textbooks I use in my introductory course on qualitative methods. Other general qualitative methods books that I particularly recommend are Patton (1990), Hammersley and Atkinson (1983), and Wolcott (1995).

Robson, C. (1993). *Real world research: A resource for social scientists and practitioner-researchers.* Cambridge, MA: Blackwell.

This book on applied research design and methods is practical, thorough, and compatible with the strategy I present here. It covers both qualitative and quantitative approaches and is the only book I've seen that explains both methods with understanding and clarity.

Marshall, C., & Rossman, G. (1995). *Designing qualitative research* (2nd ed.). Thousand Oaks, CA: Sage.

This is the only book besides mine that I know of that deals primarily with designing a qualitative study. Their approach is rather different from mine (they have lots of good examples and advice, but less of an explicit framework), and the two books complement one another.

Hammersley, M., & Atkinson, P. (1983). *Ethnography: Principles in practice.* London: Tavistock.

LeCompte, M. D., & Preissle, J. (1993). *Ethnography and qualitative design in educational research* (2nd ed.). San Diego: Academic Press.

Miles, M. B., & Huberman, A. M. (1994). *Qualitative data analysis: A sourcebook of new methods* (2nd ed.). Newbury Park, CA: Sage.

Patton, M. Q. (1990). *Qualitative evaluation and research methods* (2nd ed.). Newbury Park, CA: Sage.

All of these books have valuable things to say about design issues, although the wisdom tends to be interspersed throughout the book, rather than concentrated in one place.

Becker, H. S. (1986). *Writing for social scientists: How to start and finish your thesis, book, or article.* Chicago: University of Chicago Press.

This is by far the most valuable book I've seen on academic writing, because it bypasses grammar and punctuation and goes straight to the key issue: Why is clear, effective

writing so difficult for many people in academic settings, and what can they do about
this? It's really a book about doing research, not just writing.

Mills, C. W. (1959). On intellectual craftsmanship. In C. W. Mills (Ed.), *The sociological
imagination.* London: Oxford University Press.
The best thing ever written on what it means to be a researcher and scholar.

Peters, R. L. (1992). *Getting what you came for: The smart student's guide to earning a
master's or a Ph.D.* New York: Noonday Press.
This is the clearest and most helpful of the "surviving graduate school" books I've read.
It covers everything from deciding whether it's worth getting a graduate degree to how
to get a job after you finish. Although it's immensely valuable on the practical aspects
of researching and writing a dissertation, the specific advice on research proposals is
sometimes misleading for qualitative studies.

Rudestam, K. E., & Newton, R. R. (1992). *Surviving your dissertation.* Newbury Park,
CA: Sage.
This is different from other "completing your dissertation" books in that it focuses
mostly on the dissertation itself, rather than on being a doctoral student. It is also the
only book of this type that I've seen that knowledgeably addresses the differences
between quantitative and qualitative dissertations. It is clear, practical, and full of
valuable advice.

Locke, L. F., Spirduso, W. W., & Silverman, S. J. (1993). *Proposals that work: A guide
for planning dissertations and grant proposals* (3rd ed.). Newbury Park, CA: Sage.
Of the books I've looked at dealing specifically with proposal writing, this seems the
most helpful, and I use it in my course on qualitative research design. It's clear,
comprehensive, and practical, and it has a chapter that specifically discusses qualitative
research proposals. The advice that they give isn't limited to proposals but is generally
relevant to research and scholarly writing.

Frost, P., & Stablein, R. (Eds.). (1992). *Doing exemplary research.* Newbury Park, CA:
Sage.
The editors selected seven journal articles in organizational research that had been
recognized as important and exemplary and compiled accounts by the researchers of the
origin, conduct, and consequences of their studies, along with commentaries on each
account by experts in the field. The degree of candor here is remarkable; I know of
nothing since *The Double Helix* that gives as clear a picture of the behind-the-scenes
realities of research. It is valuable not only as a corrective to the sanitized and
depersonalized views of "good" research that permeate academia, but also as a source
of insights and models for your own research.

References

Agar, M. (1991). The right brain strikes back. In N. G. Fielding & R. M. Lee (Eds.), *Using computers in qualitative research* (pp. 181-194). Newbury Park, CA: Sage.

Anderson, G. L. (1989). Critical ethnography in education: Origins, current status, and new directions. *Review of Educational Research, 59,* 249-270.

Anderson, G. L., et al. (1994). *Studying your own school: An educator's guide to qualitative, practitioner research.* Thousand Oaks, CA: Corwin Press.

Atkinson, P. (1992). The ethnography of a medical setting: Reading, writing, and rhetoric. *Qualitative Health Research, 2,* 451-474.

Becker, H. S. (1970). *Sociological work: Method and substance.* New Brunswick, NJ: Transaction Books.

Becker, H. S. (1986). *Writing for social scientists: How to start and finish your thesis, book, or article.* Chicago: University of Chicago Press.

Becker, H. S. (1991). Generalizing from case studies. In E. Elsner & A. Peshkin (Eds.), *Qualitative inquiry in education: The continuing debate* (pp. 233-242). New York: Teachers College Press.

Becker, H. S., Geer, B., Hughes, E. C., & Strauss, A. L. (1977). *Boys in white: Student culture in medical school.* New Brunswick, NJ: Transaction Books. (Original work published by University of Chicago Press, 1961)

Berg, D. N., & Smith, K. K. (1988). *The self in social inquiry: Researching methods.* Newbury Park, CA: Sage.

Bhattacharjea, S. (1994). *Reconciling "public" and "private": Women in the educational bureaucracy in "Sinjabistan" Province, Pakistan.* Unpublished doctoral dissertation, Harvard Graduate School of Education.

Bloor, M. J. (1983). Notes on member validation. In R. M. Emerson (Ed.), *Contemporary field research: A collection of readings* (pp. 156-172). Prospect Heights, IL: Waveland.

Bogdan, R. C., & Biklen, S. K. (1992). *Qualitative research for education: An introduction to theory and methods* (2nd ed.). Boston: Allyn & Bacon.

Bolster, A. S. (1983). Toward a more effective model of research on teaching. *Harvard Educational Review, 53,* 294-308.

Bosk, C. (1979). *Forgive and remember: Managing medical failure.* Chicago: University of Chicago Press.

Bredo, E., & Feinberg, W. (1982). *Knowledge and values in social and educational research.* Philadelphia: Temple University Press.

Briggs, C. (1986). *Learning how to ask.* Cambridge: Cambridge University Press.

Brinberg, D., & McGrath, J. E. (1985). *Validity and the research process.* Beverly Hills, CA: Sage.

Britan, G. M. (1978). Experimental and contextual models of program evaluation. *Evaluation and Program Planning, 1,* 229-234.

Brown, L. M. (Ed.). (1988). *A guide to reading narratives of conflict and choice for self and moral voice.* Cambridge, MA: Harvard University, Center for the Study of Gender, Education, and Human Development.

Campbell, D. T. (1984). Foreword. In R. Yin (Ed.), *Case study research: Design and methods.* Beverly Hills, CA: Sage.

Campbell, D. T. (1988). *Methodology and epistemology for social science: Selected papers.* Chicago: University of Chicago Press.

Campbell, D. T., & Stanley, J. (1963). Experimental and quasi-experimental designs for research on teaching. In N. L. Gage (Ed.), *Handbook of research on teaching* (pp. 171-246). Chicago: Rand McNally.

Carspecken, P. F., & Apple, M. (1992). Critical qualitative research: Theory, methodology, and practice. In M. D. LeCompte, W. L. Millroy, & J. Preissle (Eds.), *The handbook of qualitative research in education* (pp. 507-553). San Diego: Academic Press.

Cohen, M. D., March, J. G., & Olsen, J. P. (1972). A garbage can model of organizational choice. *Administrative Science Quarterly, 17,* 1-25.

Connolly, F. M., & Clandinin, D. J. (1990). Stories of experience and narrative inquiry. *Educational Researcher, 19*(4), 2-14.

Cook, T. D., & Campbell, D. T. (1979). *Quasi-experimentation: Design and analysis issues for field settings.* Boston: Houghton Mifflin.

Cook, T. D., & Shadish, W. R. (1985). Program evaluation: The worldly science. *Annual Review of Psychology, 37,* 193-232.

Croskery, B. (1995). *Swamp leadership: The wisdom of the craft.* Unpublished doctoral dissertation, Harvard Graduate School of Education.

Denzin, N. K. (1970). *The research act.* Chicago: Aldine.

Dexter, L. A. (1970). *Elite and specialized interviewing.* Evanston, IL: Northwestern University Press.

Dey, I. (1993). *Qualitative data analysis: A user-friendly guide for social scientists.* London: Routledge.

Deyhle, D. L., Hess, G. A., Jr., & LeCompte, M. D. (1992). Approaching ethical issues for qualitative researchers in education. In M. D. LeCompte, W. L. Millroy, & J. Preissle (Eds.), *The handbook of qualitative research in education* (pp. 597-641). San Diego: Academic Press.

Eggan, F. (1954). Social anthropology and the method of controlled comparison. *American Anthropologist, 56,* 743-763.

Eisner, E., & Peshkin, A. (Eds.). (1990). *Qualitative inquiry in education: The continuing debate.* New York: Teachers College Press.

Erickson, F. (1990). Qualitative methods. In *Research in teaching and learning* (Vol. 2, pp. 75-194). New York: Macmillan. (Reprinted from *Handbook of research on teaching,* M. C. Wittrock, Ed., 1986, New York: Macmillan)

Erickson, F. (1992). Ethnographic microanalysis of interaction. In M. D. LeCompte, W. L. Millroy, & J. Preissle (Eds.), *The handbook of qualitative research in education* (pp. 201-225). San Diego: Academic Press.

Festinger, L., Riecker, H. W., & Schachter, S. (1956). *When prophecy fails.* Minneapolis: University of Minnesota Press.

Fielding, N., & Fielding, J. (1986). *Linking data.* Beverly Hills, CA: Sage.

Freidson, E. (1975). *Doctoring together: A study of professional social control.* Chicago: University of Chicago Press.

Gee, J. P., Michaels, S., & O'Connor, M. C. (1992). Discourse analysis. In M. D. LeCompte, W. L. Millroy, & J. Preissle (Eds.), *The handbook of qualitative research in education* (pp. 227-291). San Diego: Academic Press.

Geertz, C. (1973). *The interpretation of cultures.* New York: Basic Books.

Geertz, C. (1976). From the native's point of view: On the nature of anthropological understanding. In K. H. Basso & H. A. Selby (Eds.), *Meaning in anthropology.* Albuquerque: University of New Mexico Press.

Glaser, B. (1978). *Theoretical sensitivity.* Mill Valley, CA: Sociology Press.

Glaser, B., & Strauss, A. (1967). *The discovery of grounded theory.* Hawthorne, NY: Aldine.

Glesne, C., & Peshkin, A. (1992). *Becoming qualitative researchers: An introduction.* White Plains, NY: Longman.

Gould, S. J. (1989). *Wonderful life: The Burgess shale and the nature of history.* New York: W. W. Norton.

Grady, K. A., & Wallston, B. S. (1988). *Research in health care settings.* Newbury Park, CA: Sage.

Greene, J. C. (1994). Qualitative program evaluation: Practice and promise. In N. K. Denzin & Y. S. Lincoln (Eds.), *Handbook of qualitative research* (pp. 530-544). Thousand Oaks, CA: Sage.

Guba, E. G., & Lincoln, Y. S. (1989). *Fourth generation evaluation.* Newbury Park, CA: Sage.

Guilbault, B. (1989). *The families of dependent handicapped adults: A working paper.* Unpublished paper.

Hammersley, M. (1992). *What's wrong with ethnography?* London: Routledge.

Hammersley, M., & Atkinson, P. (1983). *Ethnography: Principles in practice.* London: Tavistock.

Hannerz, U. (1992). *Cultural complexity: Studies in the social organization of meaning.* New York: Columbia University Press.

Heider, E. R. (1972). Probability, sampling, and ethnographic method: The case of Dani colour names. *Man, 7,* 448-466.

Heinrich, B. (1979). *Bumblebee economics.* Cambridge, MA: Harvard University Press.

Heinrich, B. (1984). *In a patch of fireweed.* Cambridge, MA: Harvard University Press.

Howard, V. A., & Barton, J. H. (1986). *Thinking on paper.* New York: Morrow.

Huberman, A. M. (1989). *La vie des enseignats.* Neuchâtel, Switzerland: Editions Delachaux & Niestlé. (English translation published in the United States in 1993 as *The lives of teachers,* New York: Teachers College Press)

Huberman, A. M., & Miles, M. B. (1988). Assessing local causality in qualitative research. In D. N. Berg & K. K. Smith (Eds.), *The self in social inquiry: Researching methods* (pp. 351-381). Newbury Park, CA: Sage. (Republished from *Exploring clinical methods for social research,* 1985, Beverly Hills, CA: Sage)

Huck, S. W., & Sandler, H. M. (1979). *Rival hypotheses: "Minute mysteries" for the critical thinker.* London: Harper & Row.

Jansen, G., & Peshkin, A. (1992). Subjectivity in qualitative research. In M. D. LeCompte, W. L. Millroy, & J. Preissle (Eds.), *The handbook of qualitative research in education* (pp. 681-725). San Diego: Academic Press.

Janesick, V. J. (1994). The dance of qualitative research design: Metaphor, methodology, and meaning. In N. K. Denzin & Y. S. Lincoln (Eds.), *Handbook of qualitative research* (pp. 209-219). Thousand Oaks, CA: Sage.

Kidder, L. H. (1981). Qualitative research and quasi-experimental frameworks. In M. B. Brewer & B. E. Collins (Eds.), *Scientific inquiry and the social sciences*. San Francisco: Jossey-Bass.

Kimmel, A. J. (1988). *Ethics and values in applied social research*. Newbury Park, CA: Sage.

Kincheloe, J. L., & McLaren, P. L. (1994). Rethinking critical theory and qualitative research. In N. K. Denzin & Y. S. Lincoln (Eds.), *Handbook of qualitative research* (pp. 138-157). Thousand Oaks, CA: Sage.

King, G., Keohane, R. O., & Verba, S. (1994). *Designing social inquiry: Scientific inference in qualitative research*. Princeton, NJ: Princeton University Press.

Kirk, J., & Miller, M. (1986). *Reliability and validity in qualitative research*. Beverly Hills, CA: Sage.

Kvarning, L.-Å. (1993, October). Raising the Vasa. *Scientific American*, pp. 84-91.

Lakoff, G., & Johnson, M. (1980). *Metaphors we live by*. Chicago: University of Chicago Press.

Lave, C. A., & March, J. G. (1975). *An introduction to models in the social sciences*. New York: Harper & Row.

LeCompte, M. D., & Preissle, J. (1993). *Ethnography and qualitative design in educational research* (2nd ed.). San Diego: Academic Press.

Light, R. J., & Pillemer, D. B. (1984). *Summing up*. Cambridge, MA: Harvard University Press.

Light, R. J., Singer, J., & Willett, J. (1990). *By design: Conducting research on higher education*. Cambridge, MA: Harvard University Press.

Lincoln, Y. S. (1990). Toward a categorical imperative for qualitative research. In E. Eisner & A. Peshkin (Eds.), *Qualitative inquiry in education: The continuing debate* (pp. 277-295). New York: Teachers College Press.

Locke, L., Spirduso, W. W., & Silverman, S. J. (1993). *Proposals that work* (3rd ed.). Newbury Park, CA: Sage.

Manning, H. (Ed.). (1960). *Mountaineering: The freedom of the hills*. Seattle, WA: The Mountaineers.

Margolis, J. S. (1990). *Psychology of gender and academic discourse: A comparison between female and male students' experiences talking in a college classroom*. Unpublished doctoral dissertation, Harvard Graduate School of Education.

Marshall, C., & Rossman, G. (1995). *Designing qualitative research* (2nd ed.). Thousand Oaks, CA: Sage.

Martin, J. (1982). A garbage can model of the research process. In J. E. McGrath, J. Martin, & R. Kulka (Eds.), *Judgment calls in research*. Beverly Hills, CA: Sage.

Maxwell, J. A. (1971). *The development of Plains kinship systems*. Unpublished masters paper, University of Chicago.

Maxwell, J. A. (1978). The evolution of Plains Indian kin terminologies: A non-reflectionist account. *Plains Anthropologist, 23*, 13-29.

Maxwell, J. A. (1986). *The conceptualization of kinship in an Inuit community*. Unpublished doctoral dissertation, University of Chicago.

Maxwell, J. A. (1992). Understanding and validity in qualitative research. *Harvard Educational Review, 62*, 279-300.

Maxwell, J. A. (1993). Gaining acceptance for qualitative methods from clients, policy-makers, and participants. In D. Fetterman (Ed.), *Speaking the language of power*. London: Falmer.

Maxwell, J. A. (1995, February). *Diversity and methodology in a changing world.* Paper presented at the Fourth Puerto Rican Congress of Research in Education, San Juan, Puerto Rico.

Maxwell, J. A. (1996a). *Diversity, solidarity, and community.* Manuscript accepted for publication in *Educational Theory.*

Maxwell, J. A. (1996b). *The logic of qualitative research.* Unpublished manuscript, Harvard School of Education.

Maxwell, J. A., & Miller, B. A. (1996). *Categorization and contextualization in qualitative data analysis.* Manuscript submitted for publication.

Maxwell, J. A., Sandlow, L. J., & Bashook, P. G. (1987). Combining ethnographic and experimental methods in evaluation research: A case study. *Evaluation Studies Review Annual, 12.* (Reprinted from *Educational evaluation: Ethnography in theory, practice, and politics,* D. M. Fetterman & M. A. Pitman, Eds., 1986, Beverly Hills, CA: Sage)

Menzel, H. (1978). Meaning: Who needs it? In M. Brenner, P. Marsh, & M. Brenner (Eds.), *The social contexts of method.* New York: St. Martin's.

Merriam, S. (1988). *Case study research in education: A qualitative approach.* San Francisco: Jossey-Bass.

Merriam-Webster's Collegiate Dictionary (10th ed.). (1993). Springfield, MA: Merriam-Webster.

Metzger, M. (1993, June). Playing school or telling the truth? *Harvard Graduate School of Education Alumni Bulletin.*

Miles, M. B., & Huberman, A. M. (1984). *Qualitative data analysis: A sourcebook of new methods.* Beverly Hills, CA: Sage.

Miles, M. B., & Huberman, A. M. (1994). *Qualitative data analysis: An expanded sourcebook* (2nd ed.). Thousand Oaks, CA: Sage.

Mills, C. W. (1959). On intellectual craftsmanship. In C. W. Mills (Ed.), *The sociological imagination* (pp. 195-226). London: Oxford University Press.

Mishler, E. G. (1986). *Research interviewing: Context and narrative.* Cambridge, MA: Harvard University Press.

Mohr, L. (1982). *Explaining organizational behavior.* San Francisco: Jossey-Bass.

Nielsen, J. M. (Ed.). (1990). *Feminist research methods.* Boulder, CO: Westview.

Norris, S. P. (1983). The inconsistencies at the foundation of construct validation theory. In E. R. House (Ed.), *Philosophy of evaluation* (pp. 53-74). San Francisco: Jossey-Bass.

Novak, J. D., & Gowin, D. B. (1984). *Learning how to learn.* Cambridge: Cambridge University Press.

Oja, S. N., & Smulyan, L. (1989). *Collaborative action research: A developmental approach.* London: Falmer.

Oleson, V. (1994). Feminism and models of qualitative research. In N. K. Denzin & Y. S. Lincoln (Eds.), *Handbook of qualitative research* (pp. 158-174). Thousand Oaks, CA: Sage.

Patton, M. Q. (1990). *Qualitative evaluation and research methods* (2nd ed.). Newbury Park, CA: Sage.

Pelto, P., & Pelto, G. (1975). Intracultural diversity: Some theoretical issues. *American Ethnologist, 2,* 1-18.

Pelto, P., & Pelto, G. (1978). *Anthropological research: The structure of inquiry* (2nd ed.). Cambridge: Cambridge University Press.

Peshkin, A. (1991). *The color of strangers, the color of friends: The play of ethnicity in school and community.* Chicago: University of Chicago Press.

Peters, R. L. (1992). *Getting what you came for: The smart student's guide to earning a master's or a Ph.D.* New York: Noonday Press.

Phillips, D. C. (1987). The demise of positivism. In D. C. Phillips (Ed.), *Philosophy, science, and social inquiry.* Oxford: Pergamon.

Pitman, M. A., & Maxwell, J. A. (1992). Qualitative approaches to evaluation. In M. D. LeCompte, W. L. Millroy, & J. Preissle (Eds.), *The handbook of qualitative research in education* (pp. 729-770). San Diego: Academic Press.

Platt, J. R. (1964). Strong inference. *Science, 146,* 347-353.

Poggie, J. J., Jr. (1972). Toward control in key informant data. *Human Organization, 31,* 23-30.

Przeworski, A., & Salomon, F. (1988). *On the art of writing proposals: Some candid suggestions for applicants to Social Science Research Council competitions.* New York: Social Science Research Council.

Punch, M. (1986). *The politics and ethics of fieldwork.* Beverly Hills, CA: Sage.

Putnam, H. (1987). *The many faces of realism.* LaSalle, IL: Open Court.

Putnam, H. (1990). *Realism with a human face.* Cambridge, MA: Harvard University Press.

Quantz, R. A. (1992). On critical ethnography (with some postmodern considerations). In M. D. LeCompte, W. L. Millroy, & J. Preissle (Eds.), *The handbook of qualitative research in education* (pp. 447-505). San Diego: Academic Press.

Rabinow, P. (1977). *Reflections on fieldwork in Morocco.* Berkeley: University of California Press.

Rabinow, P., & Sullivan, W. M. (1979). *Interpretive social science: A reader.* Berkeley: University of California Press.

Ragin, C. C. (1987). *The comparative method: Moving beyond qualitative and quantitative strategies.* Berkeley: University of California Press.

Reason, P. (1988). Introduction. In P. Reason (Ed.), *Human inquiry in action: Developments in new paradigm research.* Newbury Park, CA: Sage.

Reason, P. (1994). Three approaches to participative inquiry. In N. K. Denzin & Y. S. Lincoln (Eds.), *Handbook of qualitative research* (pp. 324-339). Thousand Oaks, CA: Sage.

Regan-Smith, M. G. (1992). *The teaching of basic science in medical school: The students' perspective.* Unpublished doctoral dissertation, Harvard Graduate School of Education.

Reinharz, S. (1992). *Feminist methods in social research.* New York: Oxford University Press.

Robson, C. (1993). *Real world research: A resource for social scientists and practitioner-researchers.* London: Blackwell.

Roman, L. (1992). The political significance of other ways of narrating ethnography: A feminist materialist approach. In M. D. LeCompte, W. L. Millroy, & J. Preissle (Eds.), *The handbook of qualitative research in education* (pp. 555-594). San Diego: Academic Press.

Rossi, P. H., & Berk, R. A. (1991). A guide to evaluation research theory and practice. In A. Fisher, M. Pavlova, & V. Covello (Eds.), *Evaluation and effective risk communications: Workshop proceedings* (pp. 201-254). Washington, DC: Interagency Task Force on Environmental Cancer and Heart and Lung Disease.

Rudestam, K. E., & Newton, R. R. (1992). *Surviving your dissertation.* Newbury Park, CA: Sage.

Ryle, G. (1949). *The concept of mind.* London: Hutchinson.

Sankoff, G. (1971). Quantitative aspects of sharing and variability in a cognitive model. *Ethnology, 10,* 389-408.

Sayer, A. (1992). *Method in social science: A realist approach* (2nd ed.). London: Routledge.

Schatzman, L., & Strauss, A. R. (1973). *Field research: Strategies for a natural sociology.* Englewood Cliffs, NJ: Prentice Hall.

Schensul, J. J., & Schensul, S. L. (1992). Collaborative research: Methods of inquiry for social change. In M. D. LeCompte, W. L. Millroy, & J. Preissle (Eds.), *The handbook of qualitative research in education* (pp. 161-200). San Diego: Academic Press.

Scriven, M. (1967). The methodology of evaluation. In R. E. Stake (Ed.), *Perspectives of curriculum evaluation.* Chicago: Rand McNally.

Scriven, M. (1974). Maximizing the power of causal investigations: The modus operandi method. In W. J. Popham (Ed.), *Evaluation in education—current applications* (pp. 68-84). Berkeley, CA: McCutchan.

Scriven, M. (1991). Beyond formative and summative evaluation. In M. W. McLaughlin & D. C. Phillips (Eds.), *Evaluation and education at quarter century* (pp. 19-64). Chicago: National Society for the Study of Education.

Seidman, I. E. (1991). *Interviewing as qualitative research.* New York: Teachers College Press.

Shweder, R. A. (Ed.). (1980). *Fallible judgment in behavioral research.* San Francisco: Jossey-Bass.

Smith, L. (1979). An evolving logic of participant observation, educational ethnography, and other case studies. *Review of Research in Education, 6,* 316-377.

Spradley, J. (1979). *The ethnographic interview.* New York: Holt, Rinehart, & Winston.

Starnes, B. (1990). *"Save one of those high-up jobs for me": Shared decision making in a day care center.* Unpublished doctoral dissertation, Harvard Graduate School of Education.

Strauss, A. (1987). *Qualitative analysis for social scientists.* Cambridge: Cambridge University Press.

Strauss, A. (1995). Notes on the nature and development of general theories. *Qualitative Inquiry, 1,* 7-18.

Strauss, A., & Corbin, J. (1990). *Basics of qualitative research: Grounded theory procedures and techniques.* Newbury Park, CA: Sage.

Tesch, R. (1990). *Qualitative research: Analysis types and software tools.* New York: Falmer.

Tukey, J. (1962). The future of data analysis. *Annals of Mathematical Statistics, 33,* 1-67.

Weiss, R. S. (1994). *Learning from strangers: The art and method of qualitative interviewing.* New York: Free Press.

Weitzman, E. A., & Miles, M. B. (1995). *Computer programs for qualitative data analysis.* Thousand Oaks, CA: Sage.

Werner, O., & Schoepfle, G. M. (1987). *Systematic fieldwork.* Thousand Oaks, CA: Sage.

Whyte, W. F. (Ed.). (1991). *Participatory action research.* Newbury Park, CA: Sage.

Wievorka, M. (1992). Case studies: History or sociology? In C. C. Ragin & H. S. Becker (Eds.), *What is a case?* (pp. 159-172). Cambridge: Cambridge University Press.

Wolcott, H. F. (1990). *Writing up qualitative research.* Newbury Park, CA: Sage.

Wolcott, H. F. (1995). *The art of fieldwork.* Thousand Oaks, CA: Sage.

Yin, R. K. (1994). *Case study research: Design and methods* (2nd ed.). Thousand Oaks, CA: Sage.

Author Index

Subject Index

About the Author

Joseph A. Maxwell is Senior Research Associate at Education Development Center, Newton, MA. For 10 years he was on the faculty of the Harvard Graduate School of Education, where he taught courses on qualitative research design and methods and the integration of qualitative and quantitative approaches. Prior to this, he was a Research Associate at Michael Reese Hospital and Medical Center in Chicago, where he conducted research and evaluation on medical education, and he has taught social science theory and methods at the University of Chicago. He now has his own consulting practice. He has a Ph.D. in anthropology from the University of Chicago; his dissertation was a study of the conceptualization of kinship in an Inuit community in northern Canada. He has published articles on qualitative research and evaluation methods; combining qualitative and quantitative methods; medical education; and cultural and social theory. His present research interests include cultural theory, the philosophy and logic of research methodology, diversity in educational settings, and how people learn to do qualitative research.

APPLIED SOCIAL RESEARCH
METHODS SERIES

Series Editors

LEONARD BICKMAN, Peabody College, Vanderbilt University, Nashville
DEBRA J. ROG, Vanderbilt University, Washington, DC

Other volumes in this series are listed on the series page